you can't dance a lie
A MEMOIR OF STEPPING INTO MY TRUTH

VALERIE IHSAN

author note on gender pronouns

In my first memoir, *Smell the Blue Sky: Young, Pregnant, and Widowed*, I used the names I gave my children at birth. Since then, both of them have chosen different ones—Clover and Robert—and my oldest (Clover) uses the gender-neutral pronouns "they/them/their."

Out of respect for my children and their choices, I won't be using any "dead" names in this book and will use the singular "they" pronoun as needed.

Also, I've changed the names of some characters for privacy's sake.

*For Clover, who taught me to smell the blue sky,
So you'll know I've always tried for honesty.*

I dedicate my writings, also, to my grandmother Lola Kathleen Hanna, who wrote secretly and not so secretly. And for those loved ones that inspire me daily and who are irritated when I don't try and risk failing.

I also dedicate this book to me, as I unfold and open to the blessings everywhere.

the struggle

I yearn to fill pages with words,
With images captured on walks,
And feelings felt at my core.

Biting my lip
To get the right word
Instead of conjuring it,

I remember at the last second
To let go
To breathe
And let the word
Slide in.

CHAPTER 1

lies

Turns out the con man movies were right. I lied by telling the truth. I'd tell enough truth that the lie slipped through. And I wouldn't even know it.

Paul and I stood in the dining room on opposite sides of our Amish-made, cherry dining room table.

"You lied to me, and you *lied to yourself*," he said.

I bristled.

"How?" I said, my palms pressing against the smooth, oiled wood, grounding myself. Divorce was what I wanted. *How am I lying to myself about this?*

"Because you aren't honest with yourself. You say you want something and you say it so many times, over and over, to yourself, that you believe it. But it's a lie." His voice shook.

What an obnoxious and weird thing to say. I didn't lie to myself.

I scanned over my life in full at that dining table, like microfiche at the county courthouses back in the '90s. Fast, fast, fast, then stop—skimming and reading—then fast, fast, fast again.

Holy shitballs.
I stared at Paul through the midday light.
I did lie to myself.
All the time.

Conveniently, I mostly didn't know when I lied. But sometimes the dissonance of subconsciously knowing I was lying and not wanting to lie clanged louder than usual and my ear drums tingled and my skin curdled.

Other times, it was like a glitch in the Matrix. I'd look up and think, *Did I just say that?*

I wasn't a pathological liar. And I didn't lie to other people. Only myself.

Ah. But there was the crux of it.

When I lied to myself and lived my life based on those lies, then I *was* effectively lying to others.

I shook my head and walked away from Paul and our conversation. But I couldn't walk away from my thoughts.

I should've been more horrified that—despite not identifying as a liar—I did, in fact, lie to people (including myself) and had done so my whole life. The truth was, I was more pissed at not being a better friend to myself. It was sad, really. How could I have so mistreated myself? Lying had prevented so much happiness. Created so much pain. Scads of it. And I was about to heap even more on myself.

Looking back, I think I lied to be a Good Girl. Fear of judgment compelled me to lie.

I was thirty-nine years old when I learned to tell the truth.

CHAPTER 2

a teenager in a cult

Organized religion doesn't make people lie, but perhaps lying was my personal reaction to it. Like, *chemically*, religion and I didn't mix well. The constraints and shaming created a toxic off-gassing in me, so I lied to myself and, therefore, to others around me.

I grew up in the Jehovah's Witness cult in a small freeway town off I-5 in the Willamette Valley, surrounded by the Cascade Range, the Oregon Coast Range, and the Calapooya Mountains. Three-and-a-half decades ago, in the early '80s, we had a temperate climate. The summers would rarely go over ninety-three degrees Fahrenheit and snow was a miracle in the winter. I saw it twice as a child. But we sure had our share of rain—good for rhododendrons and keeping summer grass green, but not fun for playing outside and climbing trees. Now, it's all wildfires and heat waves and ice storms that knock out power for days.

As a "Witness," I couldn't make friends outside the congregation, but when I did anyway, the elders came one night to scold me. Instructed me on the error of my ways.

I think that was the day I started lying.

How did they even know I was friends with Jolene? We hung out at school between classes and at lunchtime and wrote each other letters. I spent the night at her house maybe twice. I went shopping with her once. We were in seventh grade.

That night, Brother Huston and Brother Grover showed up at our ranch style home on the corner of 31st and Geary Street in Albany, Oregon. It was dusk outside, so my mother closed the living room drapes. The baseboard heater below the window cast a warm current and the heavy polyester swayed.

Maybe Brother Huston's daughter, Peggy Sue—a year ahead of me in school—tattled on me. Maybe her mother saw Jolene and me at Mervyn's, buying clothes with Jolene's mother.

The elders sat across from us, my mom stiff on the couch next to me. I wonder now if she'd felt embarrassed, mortified. I bet she was furious. (But not with me.) Probably she was both. One emotion tripping over the other, igniting the other.

I shoved my hands between my knees, my insides a roiling mix of shame and defiance. Brother Huston tilted his body to the side, one hand on his knee, making room for his enormous belly.

"How is your family, Sister Todd?" one of the suits asked my mother.

He oozed with fake concern. That's how I read it.

I knew why he was there. *It's none of his business who I'm friends with.*

Except he thought it was. He was a shepherd tending his flock. I was the one causing disunity in the congregation with my behavior, showing up as a bad influence.

"We're concerned about Valerie. Choosing to associate with people that aren't members of our faith goes against Jehovah's will. He wants us to be 'no part of this world,'" Brother Huston said.

"We understand that the need for community and friendship is strong in the youth," Brother Grover said. "It is for all of us. But there are many children in the congregation that can fill those needs for you." He turned to me and waited.

My dad was watching TV in the family room on the other side of the wall, behind me. I couldn't tell which show was on.

"Do you promise to end your friendship with Jolene?" Brother Huston said.

I looked at my knees and bit the inside of my cheek, holding my breath. The couch cushions were old and soft. Just how I liked them.

How dare he? Heat radiated up the collar of my polo shirt.

When I was in elementary school and they still hand-wrote the report cards, one of my teachers had said I was a bit of a smart-aleck. My dad had words with me then. He liked respectful children that reflected well on him. Dad probably would have had a different set of words to say to these *brothers* if he could hear us.

Instead of mouthing off, I mumbled some assertion of acquiescence. (*Lie.*) I just wanted the elders to leave. (*Truth.*)

And they did, proudly nodding to themselves. Another job well done. Another soul saved.

I felt a huge dissonance growing up. The things that interested me (learning French, traveling, going to college, dating) were not the things that they *taught me* I was supposed to want (spreading the *Good News*; only going out in large groups of peers—with chaperones; dedicating my time and energy and future to God; and not wasting my life on worldly things, like careers, when I only needed to make enough money to get to Armageddon).

Since the brothers watched me for future transgressions from then on, I dutifully and tearfully explained to Jolene why I couldn't be friends with her anymore.

Peggy, the only other girl from my congregation who was close to my age and went to my school, refused to be friends with me until I fully abandoned poor Jolene and refrained from talking to her for at least two weeks. Only then did Peggy deign to sully herself with me.

I don't know why she thought two weeks was sufficient time to stop caring for someone. Maybe she thought that was enough time to punish me. Maybe middle-schoolers think two weeks is forever. It certainly felt like that to me. A two-week, forever-hell of no friends.

The Witnesses don't believe in a fiery, torture-chamber hell; when you die, you just stop. Blank. Nothingness. That's what it felt like. No Jolene and no Peggy. Nothing.

I read a lot, did my homework, and started a diary while lying across my water bed.

Because I was terrified of being shunned by the only people I was allowed to hang out with and didn't really know what I would miss anyway, I readily agreed to sign away my future and baptize myself to God. It seemed, at fourteen, the right thing to do.

I enjoyed being a Jehovah's Witness. (*Lie.*) All my friends were Jehovah's Witnesses. (*Lie.*) I enjoyed being a Good Girl. (*Lie.*) (Sort of.)

Becoming a Jehovah's Witness meant no college, no reading philosophy or other religions, no literature with fantasy, magic, or other "satanic" influences, and going door-to-door on Saturdays to "spread the *Good News.*"

When I was sixteen and seventeen and still a virgin, I did absolutely everything I could think up that wasn't actually sex.

Because sex before marriage was *fornication*. (And that was bad.)

My first boyfriend, Eric, and I had some pretty silly stories of not having sex. We did the next best, still dangerous, don't-get-caught stuff that only sixteen-year-olds raised in cults would think of.

Like driving around in my car naked. Not touching. Just driving. Naked. And laughing.

We did lots of rubbing up against each other, with Eric readjusting erections trapped in his jeans. One time he wore sweat pants to my house, and there wasn't much readjusting needed. He just poked straight up and out. So I climbed on. He picked me up, and I wrapped my legs around his waist. Dry-humping.

I had zero period at high school, which meant I went to school an hour before everyone else, and got off an hour early. An empty house for an entire hour was magic for horny teenagers. We took a shower together one time. That was a close one.

We snuggled under blankets in dark rooms and watched movies while he'd touch me, apparently under "friendly" eyes who ratted us out to the elders. Only a few members from my congregation came to our wedding the following year.

One time, while riding home from a ski trip with my family, I rested my head in Eric's lap under a blanket. *How could my parents not have known what I was doing? They had to know.* Mom and Dad were up front in the rusty blue Chevy Suburban. My two younger sisters sat in the middle bench seat, and Eric and I were in the very back.

I wasn't actually blowing him; that would've been too obvious. But during our play, I took a big slurp of Diet Pepsi and let loose the soda, letting it dribble and sizzle down his penis.

His whole body stiffened, and he grabbed my arm. I sat up, stifling a manic giggle.

"Did I just cum?" he asked, his eyes huge.

The Witnesses also taught that women, specifically wives, were not the heads of their household. Their husbands were. And while husbands and wives should always respect and love each other and decide together, the final decision would always live with the husband as the head of the household.

Hearing this repeatedly while growing up, I learned I did not get the final say in anything and wasn't allowed to have my own opinions without being ostracized. I had to hide everything about myself.

What kind of shitty future was that for an adolescent? So, in order to combat the shittiness, I told myself I preferred it that way. I told myself that it was my idea.

And thus began my journey into lying.

I lied all the time. Not to get my own way, or to look good—well, maybe that one—but *I lied to fit in.* I pretended I was someone that I really wasn't. I didn't want to go door-to-door on Saturday mornings and tell people they were going to die in a lake of fire—different from the generic Christian *hell*—if they didn't read The Watchtower and the Awake! magazines.

I didn't want to only associate with a small pool of people I didn't particularly like, just because they were on the approved list. And I really, really, didn't enjoy shunning the people I most wanted to connect with because they were a different religion than I was and, therefore, a bad influence.

However, I didn't want to get disfellowshipped—shunned myself—so I did as I was told, telling myself that actually I preferred it that way. (*Lie.*)

Whenever I was unhappy in a relationship, *I just pretended I wasn't.* That's what I did. It was how I was raised, and it's what I grew up believing.

If I wasn't happy where I was and I wasn't allowed to be where I wanted to be, then the only way to be happy was to pretend. *Pretend so hard that I believed it.*

In retrospect, I'm sure that's how I lasted so long with Paul. I *believed* I was in love with him.

CHAPTER 3

computer widow

In a craftsman-style home in the Pacific Northwest, we had a yard barely big enough for the dogs to run around, a chicken coop, a play structure for the kids, and a clothesline.

It was a Tuesday in 2007. Since Paul had the day off and didn't need to get up early, it was a no-alarm day. I woke naturally around seven in the morning. I let the dogs, Kaya and Humphrey, outside and started the coffee. Now that the kids were six and nine and homeschooled, they slept in more. As very young children—even as babies, they'd wake before six. So, getting up at eight o'clock in the morning was definitely an improvement on a no-alarm day.

Paul was in the bathroom, and the kids weren't up yet. After feeding my suburban backyard chickens and collecting their eggs, I took the opportunity to dip in the hot tub with my book. I loved the crisp mornings by myself.

We lived in Eugene, Oregon, in an uppity older neighborhood on Jeppesen Acres Road in the Ferry Street Bridge area.

We were the weird family on the street with prayer flags and a front yard garden.

I wrote after the kids were awake and otherwise occupied because I never knew when they'd get up, and I didn't like being interrupted while writing. Which sounds silly to say because, once they were awake, they always interrupted me.

The chickens murmured and cooed and ate their breakfast. They reminded me how awfully close in the evolutionary chain chickens were to dinosaurs. One chicken in particular, *Emma,* was a screecher. She was *not* nice to wake up to.

I wasn't into my soak long before Robert came downstairs. He was never one for eating breakfast, so I didn't need to hurry out. Instead, I convinced my six-year-old to get in the hot tub with me with a couple of his toy cars.

"Bring the Harry Potter book, too," I said. "I'll read to you."

He didn't want to stay in very long, though. He said it was too hot for him. So, we got out and dried off. Paul was already on the computer, playing *World of Warcraft.* He spent more time with *That Game* than he did with his family. I hated that game.

Soon, breakfast was ready, and I got the family to all pause what they were doing and come to the table.

But right after breakfast, Paul was back on the computer. It was hard to say anything about it because it *was* his day off. While I preferred for him to interact with us on his days off—as it was the only time we were all together—I understood the need for alone time and downtime and this-is-my-only-day-off-this-week-so-I-want-to-do-what-I-want time. I *totally* got that.

We'd talked repeatedly about balancing his need for computer time with family time, but it rarely seemed to make any lasting difference. I knew he loved us, but his actions spoke loudly of neglect and ambivalence. So, I did the only thing I knew how to do—I told myself it was okay as long as part of the day was with us. (*Lie.*)

Though, by lunchtime, I was fairly livid. Robert had been whiney and clingy all morning. He was bored. He was sad. He was angry. He'd bicker with me and then want to be in my lap.

I wanted us all to go on a field trip. A day trip to the Science Factory or to the park or to the library. It *was* a school day, after all.

School days were hard to stick to when Paul was home with a day off. Since he wasn't home on the weekends with us, I was totally happy to do weekend stuff with him on his days off.

I sat on the couch, and Robert promptly climbed into my lap. I gathered him into my arms and briefly rested my chin on his head. I loved snuggling with him, fully aware that soon enough, he wouldn't want me to anymore. I already had a special dispensation for touching him. He didn't like to be touched. He didn't do hugs except from me, and we forbade tickling in our house.

"Paul, I'd like for us to do something. Can you get off now?"

His fingers tapped furiously at the keyboard. Clover was watching TV beside us on the couch. On homeschool days, I limited the TV watching to educational programs. My kids were great at arguing the educational merits of particular shows, and this was one of those questionable ones. (Probably something like Franklin. The name escapes me now.) On Paul's days off, I frequently caved on the "school day" boundaries.

"Paul?"

"Can't," he said, the word whooshing out. "I'm fighting in a dungeon right now." One hand tapped staccato bursts, and one drove the mouse in erratic swipes.

"Another one?"

No answer.

There was always another dungeon.

I could take the kids by myself to the library and the park, but I wanted to spend time with Paul, too. Plus, what I really wanted was the *family time*. Not just the Paul time.

"Paul." It was like trying to get Robert to brush his teeth.

"If I stop fighting right now, I'd leave my entire party at risk. I can't abandon them."

The muscles in my neck and shoulders hardened. Paul's voice had been sharp. Condescending. He didn't like being disturbed when he was playing. It broke his concentration and caused him to mess up whatever he was doing.

But what the fuck? Weren't we supposed to be his priority? His refusal to get off the game, to set limits for himself on the gaming time, to respond when I tried to set limits for him, or to even talk to me—*to be accessible to us!*—while he was playing, taught the kids horrible things. I didn't want that kind of behavior modeled for them.

World of Warcraft was a collaborative, online game that Paul loved and dedicated his days off to, while the collaborative, real life he had with me and the kids was the one he neglected. We got the sloppy seconds. One day, he even played for thirteen hours. When kids are little, they don't even stay *awake* that long. If he wasn't careful, there would be a day when he looked up from the computer screen and his kids wouldn't want anything to do with him. He'd be a stranger to them.

Or me.

Whenever I checked in with Paul about going somewhere that morning, I never got a 'No,' but it took serious nagging and foot stomping to get him off the computer. By then, I'd had the kids and myself ready to walk out the door for ages. We were all irritated and cranky before even leaving the house.

Our time together was tainted. It wasn't a totally shitty outing, but it was subdued. It was the pleading for him to join us that rankled me. It spoiled the time we had together.

He should want to spend his days off with us.

∼

THIS WAS FAR FROM AN ISOLATED EVENT. PAUL SPENT hours a day—sometimes the whole day—playing computer games, checking out of reality. It wasn't just one day a week that I pleaded and begged and nagged, trying to get him to engage. It was years and years of it. Like current to stone, his behavior wore me down.

He played on the computer for years while I lived a life of one, grasping at the occasional day off or vacation or when he surfaced for a Date Night. But even our date nights didn't involve speaking to one another. We would go to the movies once a week.

But I didn't insist. I didn't give him the ultimatum: the gaming or me. Maybe that was religious baggage—not feeling like I had the right to go over my husband's head and demand something of him. I was good at being unaware and stuffing my emotions. (*Lie?*)

I didn't want to be a bitch, but if I had explored my unhappiness a little more, I bet I wouldn't have spent seven more years of it in a dead-end relationship. (*Truth.*)

I wouldn't call our time wasted, though.

Paul and I bought a house together after only knowing each other for three months. He adopted my children after Rob died. And he always, always encouraged my creativity—pushing me to take novel writing classes or take a semester off from school to concentrate on creating pottery stock to sell at Saturday Market.

We helped start a No Shame Theater chapter in Eugene with our theater friends and acted together. We traveled to Maui, Hawaii; Ajijic, Mexico; and cruised to the Mayan Ruins in Cozumel; got drunk on a boat (I did push-ups in front of a boatful of intoxicated people); climbed a waterfall in Ocho Rios, Jamaica; and snorkeled and parasailed on Grand Cayman island. We also drove to Banff in an RV to spread his grandfather's ashes on Beehive Mountain.

Paul worked for a company that had their own jet, and we flew to Reno on that jet, perusing museums while everyone else gambled.

We went on date nights once a week and ate breakfast out at Studio One Café every Wednesday when the kids were in school. I ate their signature French toast before I stopped eating gluten, and the yummy potato scramble after that.

We laughed, bought art, and made a life together. But it broke somewhere, and we couldn't put it back together.

My children had a father, though. They didn't before, and that was something I would never trade. Rob died when I was pregnant with Robert and Clover was twenty-two months old.

When Paul was engaged with me—with us—he was really there. Those were the times that were good. Those were the times I visualized when I felt dark and scratchy—when I felt there was no point in staying married to Paul.

CHAPTER 4

Samhain

Months later, I put the kids to bed and climbed into the hot tub with my current read. Paul stayed in to watch a boxing match. The night was dark, but early dark. Like a soft smudge of kohl under the eye. I loved my hot tub. The warmth. The alone time. The reading time.

That night I opened up *The Mists of Avalon* by Marion Zimmer Bradley, the patio sconce offering me enough light by which to read. The Celtic and pagan rituals that the characters enacted resonated within me in a surprising way.

I'd long since rejected any organized religion after my experience with it, but yearned for a way to bring the sacred to my normal world. I didn't believe in waving-a-magic-wand magic, but this novel reminded me that honoring Nature and the changing of seasons in a special way was spirituality I could get behind. Spells were basically prayers.

As a child, it did not seem out of the ordinary that cows jumped over moons, dishes ran away with spoons, or talking rats lived under rose bushes and stole electricity from farmhouses and felt bad about it. (Side note: I've always had a soft spot in my heart for the name Jeremy since reading *Mrs. Frisby and the Rats of NIMH*.) Only as an adult did I lose the magic.

I finished the novel, even reading the bibliography so I could stay in the hot tub longer. I relished the silence in the darkness, the 104-degree water sinking into my marrow, and thought about magic. About finding magic in the mundane. I thought of how I could slow down the frenetic "Mom! Mom!" of my days—the incessant carpooling, the occupational therapy sessions for my son, the errands I sped through during brief hours when the children weren't home, volunteering, potty-training the puppy, and grieving chewed-up shoes—of how I could be more present. Of how I could stop time long enough to breathe and reset.

I slipped out of the hot tub like a selkie and put on my human skin. I dried off and carried my glass of water and my novel into the house. After kissing Paul good night, I went to sleep.

LATER, IN OCTOBER, I CONSPIRED WITH A FRIEND TO bring that magic into the mundane. We planned to meet at her house for a small ritual after dinner on Halloween—me, the kids, and Paul. Just a small one. To tell the Universe, "I see you." To show the kids (hers and ours) and ourselves that, yes, the world is about to get dark and cold, but we have to go through winter so we can be reborn in the spring, like the other growing things.

We arrived, and all four kids scattered, showing off their costumes, planning candy brigades, and whooping through the house. My friend and I created a circular altar with candles and nature. Paul floated around in the back, snacking and watching the kids.

We corralled the children, and everyone sat in a circle on the floor around the altar. My friend and I handed out slips of paper to the kids and helped them write out the things they wanted to banish in the coming Celtic New Year. When I handed a paper to Paul, he shook his head.

"No thanks. That's not for me."

Heat spread to my face. I shrugged it off (*Lie*) and went back to my friend and the altar. She said nothing. I wondered if she thought he was being rude or weird. Or maybe she thought nothing of it at all.

Later that night, I checked in with Paul.

"How come you didn't do the altar with us?"

He moved around my bathroom sink to his and grabbed his toothbrush. The kids were in bed.

"It didn't feel right. Like ... blasphemous, or something."

"Blasphemous?" Paul was as close to an atheist as I knew. Why would he be worried about offending God?

"Yeah," he said, adding toothpaste. "I felt uncomfortable doing a religious ceremony for deities I don't believe in. It felt insulting to them, in a way."

"We weren't worshipping. Just doing a pagan ritual."

"But I'm not pagan."

I lifted my palms into the air and shook my head.

"You're pagan," he said. "Not me." He smiled.

I couldn't tell if he was being condescending or not. My throat squeezed.

"You can do the rituals, but they're not for me." He started brushing his teeth.

A dismissal? Was he saying, *It's fine we don't agree, but don't involve me in your little rituals?* Or did he not care enough about the topic to keep talking? Or did he not care enough about *me* to keep talking?

I brushed in silence and never brought up rituals with him

again—even though he did lots of rituals surrounding deities he didn't believe in. Like Easter. Like Christmas. I didn't grow up doing any of those holidays, but I still took part in them with him. As a family thing. As a supportive arm.

I guess that only went one way.

these are the pleasures i have known

- Water rushing and rippling over rocks in a river bed, splashing in a fountain, scraping the sand at the beach.
- Sitting in a chaise lounge on a beautiful garden patio.
- Holding hands with a lover.
- Smiling with a friend.
- Reading a talented author.
- Writing something that feels true.
- The texture of honey in my mouth.
- Seeing my children's eyes sparkle with joy and enthusiasm.
- Watching them sleep as babies.
- Seeing my dog's delight when running as fast as she can.
- Snuggling with my kids before they are too old and don't want to anymore.
- Discovering a story in a painting.
- Talking about art and the emotions it arouses in me.

- Sculpting the essence of a face and waiting for the soul to come through.
- Freedom.
- Sobbing and screaming while another held me and witnessed my grief.
- Creating.
- Exploring foreign lands.
- Feeling a part of the Divine.
- Nature.
- A sense of belonging.

CHAPTER 5

tom and jerry

On a rainy November day, with Robert in front of cartoons—Tom and Jerry—and Clover on the computer with something called Webkinz, I started some blueberry muffins for us. I loved my open kitchen. I could see everything the kids did in the living room, and I wasn't cut off from them like in our first house. The kitchen was on a whole different floor in that one.

I folded the blueberries into the batter, sounds of instrumental cartoon fighting accompanying my culinary endeavors. I removed the batter off the wooden spoon with a rubber scraper and glanced at the television. Tom and Jerry were way more violent than I remembered as a kid. In fact, all the cartoons, shows, movies, and books I consumed as a child were shockingly inappropriate.

Was that a reflection of the world in the '80s, or of me now? It didn't harm me, having watched the violence of Bugs Bunny, Wiley Coyote, and Tom and Jerry. But seeing it through a mother's eyes, when Robert tended on the aggressive side, I wondered.

I added the batter to the muffin cups and slid the pan into the oven. I set the timer and rinsed the mixing bowl, leaving it in the sink for later.

"Why do you like Tom and Jerry so much, Robert?" I dried my hands and sat on the couch next to him. It seemed to have an abnormal amount of violence in it; they were always trying to hurt each other.

"Because the little guy—the mouse—always wins!" He flung his fingers at the TV set and bounced on the couch cushion, bringing his feet underneath him. "No matter what the cat does to him," Robert said.

I wonder if he liked this underdog vision because he felt powerless. Did he crave violence because of the power it wielded? Maybe he thought if he was aggressive, people would cower before him. He would be powerful.

I hugged him briefly, because he didn't like to be touched too much, and left him on the couch. But not before watching a bit of the show myself. It felt good to sit.

That was what I should work on with him. Helping him feel powerful safely. Teaching him to read so he had autonomy in his games. Having him be more self-sufficient. Making his own sandwiches, cleaning up the living room, scrubbing a toilet here or there. Little things that created a sense of fulfillment, but also of him feeling needed. Teaching him good work.

Maybe he'd be less aggressive with others if he felt more in control of himself and his choices.

I SETTLED INTO A CHAIR AT MY COUNSELOR'S HOME OFFICE in southwest Eugene. The large windows to my right opened out to a quiet street. She handed me a glass of water and I pulled a lap blanket over my legs and sighed.

"What's up?" she said, sitting down across from me in a wicker chair. She pulled a notepad into her lap.

I hated starting with the bad stuff, but it was on my mind. And that was why I was here. To talk through my stuff.

"When I was with Rob, I knew with no doubts that he was crazy for me. We both knew we were meant for each other. That we were supposed to be together. It was immediate, right, and true," I said. I smoothed the lap blanket and crossed my ankles.

"I don't get that feeling from Paul," I said. "I don't get that he is crazy for me. That he'd battle for me. That he'd fall apart without me. That I was holding him on this planet."

Chris tucked a wisp of hair behind her ear. "Actually, I think it is true. He lights up when he talks about you, Valerie. He talks about you with a bit of awe, really. Awe that you'd come into his life."

It was mildly weird that we saw the same counselor. And I didn't know how ethical it was that she was telling me this, but I was glad to hear it. *I guess.*

"Funny thing," she continued. "It feels true to me, what he says—his feelings about you. But I *don't* get that from *you.*"

I bit my lip.

This was true. I didn't feel sick with my love for Paul. I didn't have that visceral feeling about him like I had with Rob. I didn't feel passion in my relationship with Paul. Not sexually, not romantically, not domestically, not work-related, and not with raising our kids. But that didn't mean I didn't love him. (*Lie.*) Did it?

What I had was lov*ing* and sweet and nurturing. It was an encouraging love, and we communicated pretty well, and we went on date nights and had sex when we knew the kids wouldn't interrupt us. And we snuggled and took care of each other. And we genuinely liked each other. But none of those things were passionate. Or burned. Or took my breath away. Our love wasn't the kind that unglued me, that melted my insides. The kind that took my breath away when I saw him.

And I felt tired and sad and scared of that. And impatient and restless.

When I questioned why, I remembered I had that feeling for him once.

I had fallen head over heels when we were dating and we first moved in together. But when I found out he didn't want to marry me because I wouldn't get as much monthly income from the VA, my heart broke. And I'd never felt the same about him since. I knew in my mind that it wasn't a rejection, that he was already committed, but I never quite trusted him again.

"When you heal from this," she said, "you will trust Paul again."

More than that trust, I wished to love him fully, like he deserved. (*Lie?*)

Like I deserved. (*Lie.*)

CHAPTER 6
lola

The rain soon turned to snow and our schedule was all messed up. Also, Clover was sick, so we were housebound. The week before that was Paul's vacation, and the Christmas holidays were looming. The stability of a schedule would continue to be non-existent for the entire month of December. I didn't know if I could take that. The house was trashed already.

Life was hectic and non-productive at the same time, and then my favorite grandmother—a writer who laughed with her whole belly—died. There was no funeral. No memorial. My grandfather had set up everything in his will—the money for cremation, and the burial site far away from where we lived. No fuss.

I hoped he thought he was doing us all a favor by not having to manage anything. I'd hate to think it was something more sinister. (They didn't have a good relationship.) That, out of spite, he didn't want her to be respected in a gathering of loved ones.

I had already planned on wearing purple with a red hat and

reading Jenny Joseph's poem, *When I Am Old, I Shall Wear Purple*, at her funeral. And now I couldn't.

"We can have a memorial for her ourselves," Paul said and hugged me.

"No." I sniffed and looked away.

I didn't want it to be just five or ten people in attendance, like tipping a waitress thirteen cents. All in pennies. An insult. And my grief was exhausting.

The last time I saw her in the Albany nursing home, she asked me to stay longer, but I couldn't. I had to drive back to Eugene in time to pick up Robert before the daycare closed.

"But I'll see you next week," I promised, and held her hand.

I cried on the way home, wrecked that I was letting her down so close to the end. Was she scared? Or sad?

And then she died the next evening. Before I could get back to her.

During our last conversation, she looked at me and said, "I remember you."

I've always chosen to believe she meant that we'd been in other lives together. That as she approached the veil between worlds, her memories of our other times together resurfaced.

I hoped she didn't feel alone. I hoped she saw I was there. There then, and again. And again.

CHAPTER 7
depression

I'd never been diagnosed with clinical depression. I'd never had a major depressive episode. I'd never been suicidal. And for that, I was thankful. But I had battled anxiety and depression during certain times of my life—during relationships that didn't fit me, after my husband's death, and every February. Yes. That ubiquitous and cliché, trendy Seasonal Affective Disorder. (Who named it that? Why would someone aim for an acronym for a depressive disorder that spelled out SAD? Did they think it was witty?)

I functioned. On the outside. But through so many of my years, I didn't even remotely come close on the inside. Depression and anxiety were something one pitied when I was young—something that made you broken—so I didn't talk too much about it. Also, I just felt like I was whining.

With Clover being sick and the housebound snow days, the kids had been playing on the computer for the better part of a week. I didn't know how to get them off without having a fun back-up plan. "Everybody off the computer, it's time to clean the living room!" would not cut it.

There was no safe (*read: clean*) place to be in our home right then—causing much angst within our family.

"The house is overwhelming me again," Paul said before heading off to work. "I just tried to make some toast, and I had to move seven dishes out of the way to find the toaster."

And Clover didn't want to sleep in their room anymore because it was so messy.

Sigh.

I didn't have tons of energy. Depression was an illness. I got that. But so many others had it worse than me. And I didn't feel imbalanced; I felt like a *failure*. Like, I could get nothing under control. Like, the world was spinning madly, and I was either whirling around in it, unable to right myself, or was so wet-noodle-tired that I couldn't get out of bed. Apparently, that was depression too.

In the wintertime, I liked to take it easy: drink hot liquids, use wool sweaters and quilts, knit hats, read books by the fireplace, or slip under the feather blanket and watch a movie in bed. I drew inward, as our ancestors did, bringing my work inside and quitting the fields after the harvests were done.

I also knew that if my surroundings were chaotic and cluttered, I felt that way inside. I got all sketchy and anxious. My irritation rose, and I was snippy with people and felt easily overwhelmed. Because I was a poor housekeeper, I unfortunately struggled with this frequently.

And then—in whirligig irony—there was the fatigue generated from the depression that came from being tired. It was ridiculous, really. Because it stressed me that the house was messy, I felt fatigued, and the fatigue generated a mild depression and then I just wanted to sleep. The mess in the kitchen grew larger.

I didn't ask for help often, but when I confessed my feelings of despondency, I'd get, *"But you look fine. You're doing so well,"* which always made me feel worse. They didn't believe me—which felt even more isolating somehow—which increased my depression.

On the other side of that depression, I could see that I hadn't been *honest*—with myself or others. If I'd been more open about my depression and dissatisfaction instead of martyring myself and packing my unhappiness down tightly—like brown sugar in a measuring cup—I would have saved myself much pain and years of heartbreak. (*Truth.*)

Dear Rob,

I'm visiting Massachusetts next month. I miss you. And I'm angry you are not here.

Would hugging you feel weird?

Paul is here. Is it enough? It won't ever bring you back ... but being alone won't bring you back either.

I don't feel lonely. Maybe for myself. And I miss you, but that doesn't mean I'm lonely.

This time away from my home, away from Paul, might bring clarity.

Serenity.

Bring inner peace into my space.

I want to feel through my anger, pain, and grief. Not shut it out.

Yes. I'm mad—even though Good Girls Don't Get Angry. So, what does that make me? Because I am angry.

Angry. Disappointed. Sad.

I wasn't ready to say goodbye to you. I wanted more of our life together.

I want to climb out of my skin and run through the wooded fields naked.

I still love you.

Valerie

CHAPTER 8

closure?

Out of the blue, during the following spring, an old boyfriend—Tim—randomly called up saying that he had some old photographs of mine, and did I want to meet up with him to retrieve the pictures? I hadn't seen Tim since before my children were born. Since I'd left for the Army.

The night that Tim and I became a thing, I was sitting in my little bedroom at my roommate Zach's house. My cocoon. Dark green-black walls with graffiti spray-painted in gold. It was a rule in my room that if you came in, you couldn't leave until you'd contributed to my wall art. A saying, a quote, a picture painted with false bravado.

I sat in bed, leaning against the wall, journaling. There was a tired party going on downstairs. A candle was lit at my bedside, a white taper shoved into a beer bottle. Christmas lights twinkled at the ceiling.

Tim knocked on the door frame, walked in, and closed the door. He entered with a beer in hand. Dark blond surfer wanderer. A single shell on a hemp string nestled at his throat, a hair tie around his wrist. Hard construction worker body. I craved him, but he didn't want me. Not like that. Just as a friend, he'd said. Friends were harder to come by and meant more to him, he'd said.

Tim walked to the side of my bed and looked down at me. He wobbled a little, maybe swaying. He pressed his lips into a line. His eyes looked sad.

I lifted my arm to him.

"What is it, Tim?"

"I tried to resist. But it's no use." He shook what looked like an alcohol-induced haze from his mind. "It's no use."

I sat forward and reached for him. He sat down next to me and touched my face, his fingers grazing my jaw and tangling in my hair. His lips were both soft and greedy.

Finally, I thought, and breathed him in.

Did I want to meet up with him? Of course I did. Maybe I'd never really gotten over him. But I didn't think that then. I thought I just wanted my pictures, and maybe a few "Remember when ..." conversations. It would be fun.

Tim and I planned an early lunch date a couple of weeks later. I planned for the kids to be elsewhere and drove about an hour and fifteen minutes on I-5 and Highway 34 to Corvallis, where Tim lived.

He lived in a blue, two-bedroom rental in a cul-de-sac with broken cars out front. I knocked and tried to breathe slowly. *Would it be weird? Did I look okay?*

My old friend opened the door, and we smiled at each other.

"Wow." He sighed and took my hands. "You look great, Valerie."

"'Thanks." I smiled and tinkled inside a bit at the attention. Paul didn't look at me anymore. Only at the computer.

I had dressed carefully, wanting him to see who I'd changed

into since we'd seen each other. I'd chosen a Nepalese blue-striped wrap skirt decorated with mirrors, layered over white linen pants. Blue sweater, orange scarf, and all the crystal jewelry I owned, which wasn't much—I was newly pagan.

He pulled me through the door and closed it. His place was small. A cabin. A plug-in heater with cherry coils—the kind that catches skirts on fire if you stand too close—warmed the small living room. I turned in a circle looking at his books and records, house plants, and washed dishes neatly stacked.

Tim stood back and watched me. I grinned and looked down.

I didn't really know how to be with him. Would we laugh and talk about the old days? Did we even have enough of those to look back on? I wanted to ask him about his writing, but it was too early. We'd barely even said hello.

Tim smiled. He still had the construction worker's body. His blond hair was still wavy, with only a few strands of silver. Tim approached and hugged me. He smelled peppery. He took my hands again in greeting. In welcome.

"Can I kiss you?" he asked.

"Sure," I said and grinned.

Which cheek would he lean toward? Would he kiss both, like Europeans did? He leaned in quick, but it wasn't the peck as I had imagined.

He *Frenched* me.

Damn.

A lot of old feelings surprised me then. Came up, swirling and murky. I had had no closure with him from before, when we ended. We'd never actually broken up all those years ago. We'd been living together in Albany, Oregon, in a run-down party house on Columbus Street when I left for the military. Our plans were for him to drive my car to me in Colorado after my MOS training. We would travel together from there to my duty station in North Carolina, then find a place in Base Housing to live.

But he disappeared. Stopped answering my letters. For the six weeks I went through Basic Training, his letters dwindled to nothing. He was busy, I told myself. (*Lie.*) And, yes, we had plans, but I was the one who left. Only temporarily. But still.

I never saw my belongings or my car again. Somehow, that didn't surprise me, and it didn't occur to me to ask myself why. I found out years later that he'd sold it all for drug money, saving the clothes for his sister.

Maybe the stolen car should've warned me away, but seeing him again that day for lunch triggered an avalanche of emotions in me. Excitement. Thrills and chills. Actual goosebumps on my arms.

His hand was warm on my neck. He looked me in the eyes and lingered there, waiting to see my reaction to his kiss. Had he planned this when he invited me over? Or was he overcome when he saw me, memories rising?

Could I be in love with Tim still? There was never any goodbye. I never got to neatly check off that experience in my life. You don't just shut off love. Had it been dormant all this time?

Thinking I might be in love with Tim shocked me. And shamed me. I didn't even know that it was possible to feel a romantic attachment to someone other than my husband.

I felt sick with it.

I didn't want to be romantically and sexually attracted to another man.

That was wrong.

Not to mention ridiculous. How could I be in love with Tim after one afternoon of kissing?

But we had a past ...

~

I wandered through weeks of menial home tasks, ignoring the wonder, fear, excitement, self-hatred, and curiosity. And I saw him again a couple more times, for *lunch*. Lunch, unfortunately, involved not so lunch-y activities. Mostly kissing, but—I'm so so ashamed to say—more than groping.

My feelings were finally strong enough for Tim that I didn't want to see him again until I'd talked with Paul. At least I had the conviction for that.

We were in couples' counseling by then. But it didn't feel like anything was changing at home. I wanted chickens and gardens and living sustainably and building community. I wanted help raising our children. I wanted shared responsibilities. I wanted like-mindedness. I wanted the '60s commune.

His chronic escapism was a neon flashing sign of depression, but I didn't recognize that. Instead, it seemed a personal attack on me. Or rather, the absence of attack. A nothingness. A neglect.

After years of being a computer widow, the most irritating and debilitating part of Paul's gaming addiction was not the neglect and distance; it was the waiting.

I waited and waited for years to be engaged in conversation with him, engaged in a project with him, engaged in a life with him. I was waiting my life away. Bored. Unhappy.

So.

I stopped waiting.

What about an open relationship where we would have sex with other people? It wasn't a new idea. We'd actually talked about it before, almost a year prior. So, Paul's reaction surprised me when I brought it up again, thinking we'd seriously consider it together now, in a calm conversation.

Paul sat on the edge of the soaking tub in our master bathroom, as if he had melted there. I stood next to him, my hand on his shoulder. Paul's face was ruddy, his eyes glassy. He snuffled and didn't bother to wipe away the tears when they spilled over.

I stepped up as close as I could and pulled his head to my stomach. He wrapped his arms around my waist and I smoothed back his hair as he cried.

"Okay. Okay," I said, gently shushing him like a newborn infant. "I won't do it. I won't see Tim again. And I'll never bring up an open marriage again."

The walls were white, dotted with framed Gustav Klimt prints.

"Shh." My hand stilled in his hair, sweaty with heartbreak.

But would I have even thought of an open marriage, if I hadn't questioned the rightness of us being together, or if our relationship had totally satisfied me? Why didn't I just leave him then?

CHAPTER 9
charlie

I was still interested in Tim. I didn't know why, though. He was a bit of a disappointment. Plus, I'd already told Paul I wouldn't go there. What spell did Tim weave? It felt similar to the one I fell under years ago when I first met him.

Tim talked a lot about nothing, had a noble heart, drank too much, and was interested in life.

Missed chances. Missed communication. We were the same height. I couldn't look at Paul's face when I stood next to him. My neck didn't extend that far.

In the movie (and book) *High Fidelity*, Rob, the main character, had lost a "great love" named Charlie. Rob held her on a pedestal and when he saw her again years later, he was surprised and disappointed that she wasn't the way he remembered her. That she was "as she always was all along," though he didn't notice. Until he looked back.

Maybe Tim was my "Charlie."

CHAPTER 10

keys and gravy

One day, the kids and I picked up our friend Jesse from his house. We all went grocery shopping and then, in the checkout line, I discovered that I'd locked my keys in the van. I gasped and then slumped. *Damn.*

We opted to walk home with the four grocery bags and twelve-pack of toilet paper in arms ... in the dark ... in the rain. Yes. It was raining. We did this as opposed to waiting forty-five minutes in that rain, past the dinner hour, when Robert was already doing his spirally/spinning-like-a-top thing from lack of food. (Even after we got home and the exercise that provided, he found it difficult to keep still and quiet and to stop talking non-stop during dinner.)

After dinner, the kids went upstairs to prepare for bed, and Jesse and I sat on the couch. Paul called my cell phone.

"I'm heading home from my meeting now," he said.

"Okay. Jesse and I were just starting a movie. We'll wait for you." I paused the DVD.

Thirty minutes later, Paul walked in the front door. I looked over the back of the couch at him.

"Where's the van?" he said.

I looked at Jesse, and we laughed. I had forgotten all about our mishap by then.

THE NEXT MORNING, AFTER LYING IN BED WITH PAUL, snuggling and talking in the early dark, and I impetuously and good-heartedly made homemade, gluten-free biscuits and sausage gravy (made from humanely treated pigs). Plus, a yummy pot of coffee.

No one liked the food.

I gave the gravy to the dogs and the biscuits to the chickens.

At least the animals appreciated it. The chickens! Oh, my goddess. They made the most interesting noises of excitement over the biscuits. I didn't mind "wasting" my biscuits and gravy.

I certainly wouldn't make breakfast the next day. Let them eat dry cereal out of the bag while watching cartoons on TV. They'd probably be happier, anyway.

Not that I was bitter. And the chickens loved me.

After Paul left for work, I had a glorious soak in the tub and the kids watched Saturday morning cartoons. Then Clover, Robert, and I walked down to the grocery store and waited for Roadside Assistance to unlock the van for us.

The plan for the afternoon was yard work.

Maybe.

If it didn't rain.

Maybe.

Or I could write ...

I certainly wasn't making more gravy.

CHAPTER 11
soulful and creative

I sat on a side bench at the WOW Hall on 8th Street, surrounded by the twenty-something crowd. It got noisier with each minute. The concert would end well past my bedtime, and I'd suffered an entire night of insomnia the night before. I felt decidedly like one of the oldest people in the room.

Joshua Radin's soulful voice and yearning touched me. Weeping seemed imminent. My mama talons flared, and I wanted to slice at the people talking during his performance. To sit naked to the bone in front of 50, 200, or 5,000 people and bleed with your words—open and vulnerable—deserved more respect than idle conversations barely lower than a whisper or cell phones open to texting.

The courage to do what any musician did was unmistakable and heart-wrenching to consider. I *so* wanted to have just a smidgeon of that courage for my very own.

Then, listening to Missy Higgins, I felt shame. There was no way I could ever create something as splitting-open as she could. Her voice was dynamic and alive and climbed the known spectrums. Her sound was unique, breathy and exotic.

Sometimes, during Monkey Mind Days, when my Inner-Critic was especially nasty, I wondered if my voice could ever compare to something like what Missy Higgins produced. Would I ever write anything that would carry a person's soul on currents of awareness and on quests for betterment? For Missy's songs did.

By the third song in her set, I was carried on those same currents I lamented I would carry no one on. The song was spirit-lifting, and when I closed my eyes, I was transported.

I was always in awe when an artist took raw materials, imaginings, notes, sounds, clay, paint—and turned it into something breathing, soulful and creative. Like, how did she hear the notes in her head and make them come through her fingers—into the wholeness of a song? How was that even possible? Yet that night I watched it happen. Listened to it happen.

What I love about good live music is the passion and playfulness and the down-to-earth-ness. Musicians are so real. And rare, I believe. I know it's weird to say, when there are so many of them around, but when I think of the intensity that goes into writing (my passion), and then the double and triple magic of adding the mastery of an instrument—or three—and then the courage to *perform it,* I find it truly chilling.

Their music gave me hope in humankind and made me want to continue incarnating into this lowly human form repeatedly. Especially if I could surround myself with those rare musicians who could fly.

CHAPTER 12
the gift

In the living room, Paul played an online computer game on his laptop. The children slept upstairs, and I nestled under a feather blanket in bed thinking about the movie I had just finished watching. It was a chilly night, and I snuggled deeper, trying to find warmth.

The movie's message disturbed me. *The Year of the Dog* was, roughly, about a woman who made some life-changing decisions and discovered what she was passionate about. She took action and did something about those passions—albeit sometimes in underhanded or illegal ways.

The side table lamp shined on my leather-bound journal. At least she *did something*.

I felt disgruntled, disappointed in myself, because I didn't take action. Because I didn't stand up for what I believed in. Never mind that I didn't know what it was I believed in.

I hated fear. I'd spoken to Fear before. I knew his plan. He was there to enlighten me, to get my attention, to raise the red flag of awareness. But he was an attention hog. I wanted to break his flag in two.

I hated Fear because he prevented me from feeling, from doing what I wanted, and from living the life I craved. He sucked the essence from me; I second-guessed myself. I re-evaluated and re-re-evaluated everything. Fear spoiled my life, coating it with a black-hued tinge—like tar. Ugly. I hated myself for caving and succumbing to Fear's influence—I hated my weakness.

I never feared death, really. What I feared was not living. I feared never having a passion for something. For not living with zest. For not having a cause. For not finishing something important. For not feeling important.

I stopped writing and took a long drink of water from the orange plastic cup beside me. I scanned what I'd just written and grimaced. *Just whining and ranting again.* It was hard to find words that meant what your heart yearned for. Meant what your heart *existed* for. And so I tried again, putting pen to page.

I wanted to be imbued with a driving ache—a need to do something.

I feared being a nobody, of not making a difference in someone's life. I wanted to feel alive with love and romance. Wanted to feel in love—with passion and thinking and yearning. I wanted to ache with longing. And I didn't feel I had any of that in my life anymore.

Since I was a teenager in high school, I'd wished to be passionate about a cause that I thought was worth shouting about. I'd never had one.

What if, in feeling passionate about something, I triggered a landslide—feeling that same passion for all—and it tore my organs out of my center, like gutting a deer carcass? How could I possibly choose just one cause? Gay, trans, and gender equality? Animal rights? Global warming? Universal healthcare? Green living? Schooling for children?

Poverty? AIDS worldwide? UNICEF? Habitat for Humanity?

I would burn up. Out of self-preservation, I did nothing. But then I was *not* doing something out of fear rather than ignorance and I cringed in shame at the thought, my voice stolen from my throat in punishment. My pen slowed on the page.

The darkness outside threatened the seals at the window, taking aim at my already-guilty conscience. I didn't want to live internally as a coward. I wanted to know myself as a strong woman with a fighting spirit. To have conviction.

I feared not living my life to its fullest—not using my time to follow my dreams. It was a pattern I'd noticed over the years, so I was honest when I saw it. (*Truth.*)

I looked up at the Klimt print on the wall opposite the bed. I snorted a puff of air out of my nose, laced with incredulity. I shook my head, practically rolling my eyes at myself. I *had* a dream. A *passion*.

To pursue a full-time writing practice and career.

Earlier that week, Paul and I went to the $1 theater to see *Dan in Real Life*.

"It would give me great pleasure to give you exactly what you need to write," Paul said as we crossed the parking lot. "It's so much easier to not live your dream and always say, *If I only could.*"

In the car on the way to the movie theater, he'd encouraged me to stop working at the health clinic's front desk in exchange for a discount on my massage room rental. I wasn't earning much money anyway, being new to my massage license and having no clientele. Quitting at the health clinic meant I could live my "writerly life o' dreams," as Anne of Green Gables called it.

He shifted in front of me to open the glass door of the theater, then followed me in. We were running a bit late.

"It's easy to blame other things and people for what you don't do. If you don't become an artist, you can't fail as an artist. You don't have to fear failure if you never try it—it's easier to make up excuses," Paul said.

"*I would've been great if only I would've done it,*" he generalized. "Some people create excuses for why they don't do things because that's easier than doing it and risk not being great. So I want to take away all your excuses."

He smiled and winked, and I bought him a ticket. I was dying for popcorn and the buttery salty aroma seduced me closer to the concession stands.

So, instead of filling my days with busy work—errands, volunteering, meetings, housework that I could do at other times—I had asked for and received the most valuable gift. Time. So what was I going to do with it?

Would I waste it? Discover other things to volunteer for because now I had time? Become a master housecleaner to avoid writing? (Probably not.)

Would my fear of being a terrible writer prevent me from trying? Would the people who read my work secretly hate it and pity me because they thought I didn't know how bad of a writer I was?

Would I play too much? Selfishly hoard and stake out time for myself when one day a week would suffice? *Would my family suffer because of my choices?*

The questions plagued me, even as I wrote them down in the journal. They created a sticky web of self-doubt I feared would pin me down ever more. I took a deep breath and shifted in the bed, bringing my knees up and the journal closer, dislodging the negativity, and shifted to pragmatism.

Mostly, I hated being afraid because it was such a waste of energy and time. I had no one to blame but myself—which didn't make me any happier. It was a bummer to blame myself for things. Especially when I deserved it.

Yes, it would be scary. I would either succeed or I wouldn't. I could no longer use the excuse of not having time to prevent my fear of failure. I needed to try, and maybe fail. And for that, Paul was happy. Not that I might fail, but that he had created the space for me to try.

Trying and failing was better than not trying and not failing. Because that was cowardice. That was not living. That was living in fear.

CHAPTER 13
i didn't fit

I climbed into bed. All the kids and dogs were in bed too—Humphrey in the crate next to me, Kiya upstairs with Aniela. I settled in, propped up with pillows, and lifted my sweatshirt to cool my belly from the feather blanket atop me.

I felt like I was on the brink of something.

There was a line from a movie—*Proof* with Gwenyth Paltrow—that rang through me.

"I feel like I could crack open. Like an egg. Or that stinky cheese that oozes out of the crust."

Paul told me he enjoyed being able to take away all my reasons for not being a full-time writer.

Should I jump? Leap? Risk sounding foolish? I just didn't want to waste my opportunity. I'd be so disappointed in myself. And Paul would be, too. Disappointed in me.

Disappointed sounded like such a vague, vanilla-bland word.

Vomit. Pink and sour on the concrete beneath my sneakered feet. *That* was how I'd feel about myself if I didn't try.

Succeed or fail. Either. Just one of them. Or both. It could be both. I wanted it to be both. For every failure, every rejection letter, would get me closer to success. Rejection equaled success.

Crack open.

Be real.

Be here and ugly and beautiful and jagged and raw and eye-opening and poignant and trespass on the should and report reality through emotions.

Sometimes I didn't feel quite like I fit in Paul's life, a leftover puzzle piece. But other times, like tonight, I felt full of wonder and thankfulness at being with him. He encouraged me like no other had done. He believed in me. Me.

My, my. I hadn't thought of that before.

I believed in reincarnation and energy medicine and enjoyed pagan rituals. He was an atheistic, existentialist humanist. But we both liked Nature, books, movies, and living passionately with authenticity.

Maybe I could make this work.

CHAPTER 14

a morning moment

One morning, I started up the stairs to wake my children, but I stopped. I wanted to take their pictures while they slept. I hadn't done that since they were infants, save once on a road trip when all three kids (Paul's daughter, Aniela, was with us) were sleeping in the van with their mouths open.

I doubled back to grab the camera and tiptoed across the tan shag carpet to Robert's bed.

I fixed the frame on him and clicked. Blurry. I tried again. Nice and clear, but off center. I tried a couple more times and by the time I'd clicked about five or six, Robert moved for the first time.

"Mom!" he said, with his eyes closed. "I said I didn't want my picture taken while I'm sleeping!"

His eyes were still closed.

I turned off the camera and clambered onto the soft bed.

"Oh. I'm sorry. I thought you said you wanted me to." I tucked the blankets around him and snuggle-kissed his cheek and head and forehead.

He smiled and giggled. His eyes fluttered open, one delayed with morning stickiness.

"I said if I was half on the bed and half off," he said.

We'd had a conversation the day before about this very thing because yesterday's morning wake up showed his special warm snuggliness peeping out from above the tangled covers. And oh, how I wanted a picture then. I remembered a previous wake up when my son re-situated himself under the warmth after having put on his clean shirt.

"I love blankets, Mom," he sighed.

Today, I touched his wild hair, and the dog flopped down on Robert's feet. On the bed. She was hard to scold because she was a love and part of our pack. Robert also loved her in his bed because he was lonely at night. I considered buying a king-sized bed so we could institute the Family Bed. Even at Robert's late age. Seven years old.

In Clover's room, I changed their CD from room-soothing-sleep-music to a quasi-rock band they liked, and snapped a picture. No movement. I got closer and centered the shot right on their angelic face. *Angel Baby*. (At ten years old.) And snapped again.

"I was awake after the first one," they said, with complete affect and deadpan droll.

They rolled over, stretched, and yawned at the ceiling. "The flash woke me."

And so my morning started. I loved my children. They were inspiring reincarnations of souls I'd loved over and over. What bliss.

CHAPTER 15

parallel lives

Over the next year, because I needed community—especially since I wasn't getting it from Paul—I filled the house with scouting meetings, hot tub parties, and invited a roommate to live with us. Paul didn't join me in any of this. Except for agreeing (begrudgingly) to the roommates. He simply was never home, and when he was home, he was on the computer playing video games.

I wanted to live a life of meaning, so—with help from my Master Gardener roommate at the time—I smothered the yard with cardboard and wet leaves, killing the grass and planting that front yard garden instead. My roommate was the one who built the chicken coop while I raised chicks in the garage. I wasn't emotionally or romantically attracted to my roommate, but we had more in common than Paul and I did. And that was weird.

Despite our dissolving connection, Paul and I still stayed in the same orbit as each other—if not tethered anymore—but I was still needing things Paul wasn't giving me. Companionship, shared parenting, as much intimacy as I craved, or even shared life goals.

In the evenings, I started watching movies in bed alone while Paul computered in the living room. We never went camping or on day trips or overnight to Portland because he'd always worked every weekend, and mostly only ever had six days off per month if he was lucky. I hated his job and the hours it took him away from us. I campaigned to get him to quit for years, but he never would. He liked his job.

Every day, for more days than I could count or remember, I'd get up, take the kids to school or homeschool them, depending on the year, slog through mountains of housework, and think about ways to be happier.

I wasn't happy with Paul. That was the truth. But I could never say it aloud, even to myself. It was a whisper deep inside that I refused to acknowledge. We *did* laugh together. Sometimes. Paul was a good man and a good father, and we shouldn't leave good men.

My mom once shared with me how she'd told her father that she was unhappy in her marriage to my dad. His response?

"Does he beat you?"

"No," my mom said.

"Well?"

And that was the end of the conversation. A polite 70s form of, *If he's not actually hurting you, suck it up.*

Paul had never come close to any sort of abuse. He never ever would.

Did that mean I was doomed to a shadowy existence, half alive, always wanting and waiting? (*Was emotional apathy neglect or abuse?*)

I couldn't leave Paul because I'd made a commitment to my family, and I stuck with my promises. If I could convince him to open up our marriage, even though I'd told him I wouldn't bring it up again, I could date other men. Then the burden of my unhappiness wouldn't fall only on him, and he wouldn't feel devastated about me leaving. And Paul clearly didn't have time for me.

In an open marriage, I could fill in the blanks.

Or so I thought.

the way it was to write

I dreamt about writing when I slept.
When I woke in that dreamy half-sleep, I thought of
    the things I was going to write about. The things I
    had to say.
To the world,
To my self,
To my friends.
To my not friends.
To the friends I hadn't met yet.
I didn't think I had any enemies, but if I did, then to
    them, too.
But when I fully awoke and settled into my journal, or
    the computer, other things got in the way.
Other emotions blocked my writing
Behind a barrier of 'what ifs'
and the bricks of 'you're not good enough.'

CHAPTER 16

my writing space

A year later, the house smelled of brownies.

Our new roommate was cooking lunch and my kids had friends over. Robert and his new friend were playing video games in the living room in front of me. Clover and two others came in from playing outside to remove the brownies from the oven.

I tried writing at the dining room table. Sometimes my writer friend Julian would come over and write with me. We met him at the theater group, No Shame Eugene. But today it was just me and all the surrounding noise.

The sounds of my house at that moment included: water running from the kitchen sink, my son singing to himself, laughter, conversation, the oven door closing, the digital timer being set, the keyboard letters depressing under my fingertips, the kids' feet stomping up the stairs, a fork scraping the bottom of a skillet on the range top, the dishwasher running, the oven heating again from when the kids put the brownies back in because they weren't quite done.

Something fell on the floor.

One kid munched a raw carrot and the other children cut the too-hot brownies. My roommate opened the refrigerator with intent, and began to empty the moldy, rotten food that we'd waited too long to eat, dumping it into the trash.

"I can sound like a goat," my oldest informed one guest.

"I can sound like a pigeon," he countered.

More laughter.

This was before I knew of noise-canceling headphones. I loved that my kids were engaged and playing and learning, but the noise was frustrating when I was trying to write.

My house was full of enchantment and experiences and clutter and toys and dogs and dirt and paper art on the walls. Also quotes and lists and bulletin boards. A friend once said this was hard to look at. That if I took all the scraps of paper taped to the kitchen cupboards down, the Qi would flow better. It would feel less scattered. That then *I* would feel less scattered.

What she said made sense, but I liked the lists and quotes that reminded me to treat my children with love and kindness and respect. Reminded me of the holiness and divinity within myself and all that I met. Reminded me to eat all my vegetables, and which foods had protein in them. The drawings that showcased my children's brilliance in art—reminding them they were loved and important and capable of greatness. Reminded me of small things I could do to save the planet. Reminded me how to build community.

The clutter that bothered me, that affected my mood and created those stagnancies of energy in the house, were the paper collections on horizontal surfaces that grew vertically at alarming rates. The pile on top of the stereo, Japanese flash cards and dictionaries and a sewing calendar. The pile by the back door, bills and phone numbers and scratch paper and pens and markers that spilled out of their jar. The pile on the bar, old science dioramas, a laptop case still fresh in its packaging, laundry hung over bar stools for drying, homemade candles and more paper of unknown origin.

The writing space I envisioned in my head was so completely different from what I actually saw before me that *to say it was laughable* would be cliché and ... laughable.

The writing space I wanted was mostly silent. Maybe a room with a breeze blowing white gauzy curtains and no paper on the walls or flat surfaces. One where the children weren't playing Apples to Apples with friends or squealing at the Xbox 360. One where the puppy didn't ring the jingle bell hanging from the back doorknob to let me know he wanted to go outside. Or where the dishwasher didn't remind me that another load needed to be done, or the laundry piles in the laundry room didn't remind me I still needed to pack for an upcoming trip.

My imagined writing space would be a place of silence and harmony where distractions were minimal and where I could access that section of my soul that knew what needed to be written. The key would unlock with a delightful click and the room I entered would be fresh and I would write what I saw.

The dryer buzzed.

I put away the laptop. There would be no writing today.

CHAPTER 17

Tamara

Fall arrived again with a dreariness that I recognized. I wanted more friends, and a knitting circle in the living room sounded just the right amount of *hygge* cozy.

The night I met Tamara, she came over with a mutual friend to knit. It was just the three of us that night, and Tamara and I hit it off. We'd had some similar life experiences with creativity, men, and cults (her mom raised her as a Mormon), and we started emailing and calling each other.

She lived out of town, in West Fir, with her husband and three children. Her three kids were all under five years old—the youngest was an infant, only months old.

A few months into our friendship, she left her toddlers and the baby with a sitter for the first time and came to see us. She and I and Paul sank into the hot tub, and she lit her one-hitter.

"So I'm just going to tell you all my shit, so that all the other times I see you I can just say, *No change*," Tamara said. "Okay?" She blew out a puff of marijuana smoke, waving it aside as she gestured.

Paul and I nodded, and I lowered my shoulders under the

104-degree water.

She was struggling with her husband. He was abusive in more ways than she wanted to admit, but she did the same soldiering on that many women in domestically violent situations did.

I didn't know the extent of it or I would've become more involved. But, as it was, I could provide friendship and a place to soak her cares away. I'd only known her a short time, but we definitely clicked.

Our friendship made sense. Two sides of the same cult coin. Later we would become soul sisters, sharing Power of Attorney and house keys. Later still, she became a beneficiary in my will.

I'd lost touch with my family for a while, and Tamara became mine. Tamara's family was abusive, so I became hers.

A week later, Tamara called me.

"Remember when I told you all about my worries and my life and Matt stuff? And I said I wanted to do that so that I could just say, *No change* every time I saw you after that?" she said.

"Yeah."

"Well. There's been a change."

I chuckled. "What happened?"

"He threw me out."

I opened my eyes wide in their sockets.

"What?" I moved out of the living room and stepped outside for some quiet.

"Well, we fought," she said. "He said he wanted a divorce."

"What happened?" I whispered.

The line went silent while I waited for her to continue. Maybe she was struggling with what to say. Maybe she was embarrassed. Maybe she was sad.

"He kicked my four-year-old."

I gasped.

"Oh, my god. Is he okay?"

"Yes."

I pictured her hands shaking or fumbling for a cigarette. I didn't even know if she smoked tobacco, but *my* hands were shaking.

"After he did that, we fought. I followed him upstairs, and I slapped him. I did. I slapped him." Her voice hitched and her breath huffed in the telephone receiver. "He kicked my four-year-old toddler."

She was crying now. I could hear it. Maybe I was crying, too. Or maybe I was cold. Hyper-alert. As I usually was in a crisis.

"What happened next?"

"He hit me," she said.

A surge of protectiveness flashed through my sternum, hearing the shame in her voice.

"I jumped on his back and started choking him with my arm. Hard."

I walked to the play structure and sat in the swing, pushing my feet into the grass, anchoring myself.

"He managed to say *I can't breathe,* and I let go. Raised my arms. Slid off his back." She was silent for a long time after that.

I lifted my feet and let gravity swing my body a bit. Tamara finally sniffed. I could hear a lighter flick.

I cleared my throat. "I'm still here," I said.

She knew, but maybe she needed to hear it.

"We left each other alone for a bit after that. But by the end of the night, he said he wanted a divorce. He said he was leaving and he couldn't spend another night in the house with me. He went to a motel."

I sighed. "Oh, man."

"I stayed in a friend's trailer in Oakridge last night, but I can't keep staying there. The only way I'll be able to get a job and be a supportive single mom—" she gulped, "—is to be in Eugene."

She took a deep breath and blew it out.

"I don't know what to do," she said.

"Well, I do," I said. I stood up from the swing. "You can stay here."

"What?"

"Yeah. Steve moved out to have more room for him and his daughter. It's empty right now. You can have it as long as you need."

She chuckled nervously.

"And I'd love your company," I said. (*Truth.*)

Tamara only ended up living with us on the weekends. She and her ex shared the West Fir house so the children could stay in one place at first. Just until they finalized the divorce. She would leave the house in West Fir on Fridays when Matt showed up and come to me.

I loved sharing coffee with her in the morning and having someone to talk to in the in-between times. She'd leave on Mondays and go back to the children for the week.

Soon enough, she found a three-bedroom home at a co-op in the Whitaker neighborhood in Eugene.

And I missed her.

I missed the distraction of her. I didn't have to think about me and Paul when Tamara was around. (*Truth.*)

Plus, asking her to move in was the proudest Friend Moment I'd ever had. Even since. Sure, it was a Good Deed, but I really felt like I made a difference in Tamara's life that day, and the days that followed. She certainly had made a difference in mine. Offering her refuge cemented our friendship.

Maybe that was the day we became family.

CHAPTER 18

magenta-flecked puce

I drove my kids to a hiking trail near waterfalls and met up with Clover's scouting group to work on their Hiking badge and Direction Finder award. It was raining and though it was a pleasant hike and I loved watching the children interact, as well as connecting to some adults I admired, the trip was way beyond my exhaustion level.

When depression pressed down on me, I usually wanted to sleep. In fact, that was what gave me the heads-up that I'd entered the blue phase. Though why it should be called blue—which evoked healing and calmness and serenity—baffled me. It should be called the *puces*.

Puce was that sickly mustard blah color that better depicted the flaccid jelly I became when in the doldrums. Magenta also seemed an appropriate color to augment the *puceness* of my state when depressed. Magenta-flecked puce.

Magenta screamed and overwhelmed the senses and deviated from any normal protocol. It was the color of anxiety.

Sleep seemed so blissful in my magenta times. During my magenta puce times, I just wanted to sleep.

We humped back home from the hike, stopping for cocoa with whipped-creamed straws and decaf coffee, dealt with parental disciplinary actions at home, and then went to a friend's house for dinner. By bedtime I was magenta. After exchanging stories with Paul about our day, I rolled over in my bed, completely puce.

The next day, the kids and I cleaned their vile bedrooms for *hours*.

With both their bedrooms beautiful, there was a sense of accomplishment in the air and we went to Chuck E. Cheese's to celebrate.

After a couple hours of reading, I looked at my watch and then found my kids. Robert was sitting in one of those motorcycle racing games, probably thinking he was really playing, though I hadn't given him any quarters.

Clover looked over his shoulder, ever watchful of him. I worried Clover felt *too* responsible for Robert. Clover was too young to worry like that.

"You guys ready to go?"

"No!" they both said in unison.

"Okay, but I'm getting pretty tired. I'd like to go soon. Thirty more minutes. Okay?"

"Okay!" they said together again, like twins. The two raced off toward the primary-colored tunnel maze.

While I waited, a housekeeping list plagued me until I wrote it down.

If I dedicated one day to each section of the house and excluded the days we had out-of-town guests or plans that took more than half the day (and maybe a day off once in a while for good behavior), I could be done with a major house cleaning *in seventeen days*.

I didn't know if I felt excited that I might be on top of things finally or further depressed that *One*, it could actually take seventeen days to clean my house, and *Two*, that at the end of said seventeen days I would have to start all over again.

The puce rolled in again.

But wait. With a couple of game plans and my newly completed list, plus a successful day of cleaning behind me, I could see the magenta-flecked puce fading and while it *was* time to get the kids home and to bed, I wasn't crabby and ready to hibernate for twenty-one days like yesterday.

Unless, of course, I spied the kitchen on the way to my bed that night.

CHAPTER 19

writing time

My work time/writing time was from 10 a.m. to noon. That was the rule at home. I wrote, and the kids left me alone unless there was blood or fire. Some days, it didn't work so well.

I HAD A STRANGE DREAM LAST NIGHT.
You know what I would do if there was an earthquake?
Can you do the closure on my bra?
Then the dog stepped on my foot.
You know why I love the internet?
And in my dream I: (insert HUGE story here)
Could you get the stuff ready for me to clean the back door? I can't find the vinegar.
I'm hungry. I'm not saying you have to get up right now and get me something. I'm just saying that if I get too much more hungry, I'll get a bit grumpy.
Yaw-Hoo! Yea, baby! Uh-huh, Oh Yeah! (exclaiming over the computer game my son is playing)

I take it the dishwasher is clean.
I would wait except for the fact that I'm so hungry it hurts!
Poison Arrow! (more computer gaming) *Booya! Poison, poison, poison, poison, poison!*
Will you stop chanting poison?
What? It's a poison arrow. (pause) *Fine.*
Two slices of deli meat.
Deli meat? What do you mean deli meat?
Turkey.
Oh.

CHAPTER 20
follow the leader

In my life, I was both a leader and a follower.

Sometimes I grasped the energy whirling around me and harnessed it into forward momentum. I gathered resources and charged forth with passion and discernment. I knew what needed to be done, and I did it. I knew where to look for answers, and I knew what steps to take to get me what I wanted.

Years ago, a friend said, "You amaze me. You say you want a dog kennel built on the side of the house, and the next time I see you, it's there. You did it."

"Why would I say I want something and then not make it happen?" I said. It didn't seem logical to me. But that must have been my sowing and reaping time. My leader time. For now, I felt fallow. My follower time.

I still felt the surrounding energy, the potential for the fantastic, but I didn't seem to harness it anymore. For now. For now, I was the follower, but I didn't like that feeling. I didn't like that place I had somehow put myself in. Right now, I didn't feel like I could make a dog kennel materialize.

I remembered Saturday mornings in the house I grew up in.

I remembered sweatshirts and coffee mugs and spiral-topped steno pads with lists, of the stereo on and the windows opened.

I remembered my mom's challenge to tackle the house and strip it of its clutter and filth, of its resentful and mocking attitude.

I would answer her call, and we would leap forward with purpose and a destination. We would conquer the negativity that clouded around us, and we would then breathe fresh air and Lemon Pledge.

We would see shiny surfaces and spread clean sheets and set the timer for forty-five minutes so we could switch the laundry out. And we would have the knowledge that we succeeded. We overcame the Other Entity, the house, that would sometimes overcome *us* to live its own agenda. Sometimes I wondered if it was trying to drive us out.

When I felt weak and overwhelmed at my home's "agenda," I longed to capture that same spirit my mom had. To devour the negativity. To banish the stagnant energy and to breathe fresh air again. But my mom wasn't there. She lived in Washington state and I couldn't answer her call to arms. I must do the leading, and not the following.

But I didn't know how. The house, the Other Entity, was winning. Old manuscript pages covered the floor at my feet, dirty dishes cluttered my writing desk, books lay on the floor. Baskets, canvas bags, one shoe, a pair of scissors, one of Paul's shirts, and a pair of faerie wings. That was just my office.

Crossing the threshold into my home, the following would accost you: a memory foam mattress pad that needed to be returned to Bed, Bath and Beyond, the other shoe, the remains of a bag of kitty litter I needed to spread under the motorcycle that sprang a gas leak yesterday. Two coats and a poncho that fell off the coat rack, a pair of slippers, and Robert's flip-flops. Also, a placemat on the stairs.

The living room, dining room, and bar all had their own piles of clutter and filth. The kitchen was unspeakable. All of our bedrooms and the back patio fell into that category as well. Hysteria bubbled up within me.

What do I do?

Where should I start?

In frustration, I usually started with a list. A plan of action. A room to start in. But without my mom to call the battle cry—to *lead* the assault—I couldn't seem to get past putting on a bandana and drinking three cups of coffee. I had no one to follow.

CHAPTER 21

the muse doesn't watch msnbc

My Muse seemed on vacation. Or taking a nap. She certainly wasn't there with me while I was trying not to think about making dinner in a half hour for four children, who then needed to eat it and be driven to a different house so that I could go to my theater workshop.

So where was this Muse? Where did she live? Did she even have a home? Or did she flit from place to place, inhabiting artists the world over?

Somehow, I pictured this to be true. If we opened ourselves up to the Muse, we allowed her to do her magic, and then we created visionary work. Or at least editable work. If we blocked the Muse from working her stuff, we didn't get the juice, and then no one else could either. She stayed there, working on the unwilling recipient, until an inkling sank in before she could move on.

The faster she could dance the inspiration in, the faster she could move to the next artist. We had a *duty* to our fellow artists to be open and willing to receive at all times.

I was listening to Pakistani rock music, hoping to dislodge

any walls mistakenly erected, preventing Musey from getting in. You know, like a surprise tactic.

Paul was freaking about the economy. It looked fairly grim that year, if you observed it in financial snapshots. For instance, Anna (Paul's 65-year-old, newly retired mother) lost $16,000 in stocks in one day. *Gulp.* That was enough to stop the boat.

Both Paul and Anna attached themselves to MSNBC. It was on all the time, a terrifying, and conversely, annoying, reminder that we were not in control of our lives. Let alone our finances.

I, however, was not watching the TV. I wasn't listening to the news. I wasn't looking. I didn't know if I was being naïve or positive. I think I was just waiting.

I reminded Paul that we had been mentally preparing for this eventuality for years. I emphasized the word *mentally*, as opposed to physically, because we hadn't been able to build respectable savings; we hadn't stopped buying books by the truckload; we hadn't stopped eating out; we hadn't stopped going to counseling or buying organic food. We hadn't stopped living beyond our means.

But we talked about it.

We made elaborate budgets and didn't keep them. We dreamt of buying another rental property, selling off the two houses we already owned and paying off the mortgage of the new rental to live in it mortgage-free. We'd even planned for a day when Paul would leave his job and the dying industry he'd been in for thirteen years and become my personal assistant. Really. That was actually one of his dream jobs. And, *dude,* I was all over that.

He thought he wanted to be Mr. Mom.

"Honey, did you forget you have your writer's group tomorrow night? You have something written, right? No? Why don't you just take off? I've got the kids. I'll get their bath ready

and put them to bed—you go to Brewed Awakening, get a nice latte and write."

That totally would've been my dream job for him, too.

The downward spiral of the economy was really a blessing. It brought us closer to our dream life. Yes! Paul could've gotten *laid off.* How was that for looking at the bright side?

I guess Miss Muse did drop by for a bit after all, but maybe it was just the Pakistani music.

CHAPTER 22

reaching out

One evening after watching a movie, I felt uplifted. Energized. The movie was about dreaming big and making it happen; and love and individuality; being recognized and admired. I felt so good, I didn't want to go to sleep immediately, so I went out to the living room and kissed Paul.

I kissed him again and again, with tongue and sighs and murmurings. And as soon as I lifted my head, Paul looked down at his laptop and continued playing his video game.

I tried for lightness.

"Second string again. I don't like this."

I gathered the DVDs together to return the next day and noticed a quirky, and what I thought was a sexy smile.

"What's that smile for?" I grinned.

"It feels like you are trying to see how long you can keep me from my game. Like you're playing your own game," he said.

A coolness slipped in where warmth and hope had been only moments before.

"No," I said. "Just reaching out. And I didn't get a response. And that makes me sad."

He said nothing. Just kept playing.

I walked away and crawled into bed alone.

He once told me—when open marriage was a hypothetical and not a request—that I could have sex with other people as long as it didn't interfere with our relationship. He wouldn't feel jealous as long as his time came first. Paul wouldn't wait for me while I was with someone else.

But would he even notice?

I shouldn't need to *convince* myself to love him; our love should be a part of me, as essential as breathing.

I had every intention of succeeding at our happily ever after. But what if, despite communication and creativity, it didn't work? What if we just didn't have the foundation of love beneath?

How could I tell if this was really love (*Lie*), or if I just wanted it to be? Was I tricking myself? Was Paul?

Of course, I loved Paul. I cared for him. I had compassion for him. But did I love him, love him? How could I tell? I was so sure at first, but more and more frequently, I'd wake up and wonder if I loved him.

Some days it didn't feel like it, and that horrified me. On so many levels. The choices were all sickening.

- Realizing that I didn't love him, and in doing something about it, I would have to alter so many lives;
- Realizing that I didn't love him, deciding not to say anything and living with it for the rest of my life;
- Wondering, if I had felt so sure before, why my mind would trick me; or

- Thinking I loved him but feeling such indecision and hopelessness. And, if that was the case, *why? What was wrong with me?*

The really disturbing part was I didn't know what to do about any of it. I felt stalled, like I was in purgatory. And I didn't believe in purgatory.

CHAPTER 23

velociraptor

One day I was crying and journaling and deep in my process. When I turned the page to finish writing some vital point, I found a velociraptor sticker lodged in the crease of my journal from my son's collection—and my thought scurried out the window and evaporated skyward.

I felt a strange mixture of lightness and sorrow.

Lightness because it was pretty silly to see the dinosaur peering out at me from the pages of my journal like I'd caught him taking a shower.

And sorrow because it seemed to always be that way. Just before I connected to Spirit or Muse and learned something vital to my personal growth, I faltered because of dinosaur stickers or my son greeting me home before I even got out of the car because I was trying to steal a few minutes in the driveway to compose myself and journal after a counseling session or just because I felt too drained to journal and watched a movie instead.

Paul and I were not drifting apart, but—

What's the word where in ancient times, in war, the city dwellers would fortify the forts; prepare for battle; and get ready for a rough road ahead? I sensed that Paul and I had done that, or we were getting ready to.

We needed couples' counseling, but I was too afraid to do it for real. Afraid to hurt Paul. Afraid to get into a conversation or situation with Paul in counseling that created an irreconcilable divide and forever altered our relationship.

My head hurt all the time. I avoided my kids. I avoided Paul. I avoided myself.

I wonder what my writing group would say if I wrote about this. My writing group meant Paul's mom since she was in the group.

After I got home from yoga class the next day, Paul left for work, dropping Clover off at school. I made myself and Robert an omelet for breakfast, and we played with Photo Booth for a bit. Then I unloaded the dishwasher, started a new load, wiped down counters, and started a load of laundry.

A sigh shuddered through me. My crushes were just fantasies, and I needed to be loyal to Paul, because ultimately, that'd bring us closer.

Or was that a cop out?

I scrubbed my bathtub and put Robert in it for a bath. He played with toys in the bubbles while I wiped down the dining room table and picked up Xbox stuff in the living room.

The truth was, Paul did not satisfy me. But what if it was *Me* who didn't satisfy me?

I straightened the coffee table and looked around the room. Maybe my marriage depended on creating art. My artistic endeavors provided diversity and challenge and prevented boredom.

A couple of hours later, I started some tomato soup on the

stove top because Robert only ate cheese sandwiches dipped in tomato soup these days. It's all he ever wanted for food.

I checked in a couple of activity books to get some inspiration for a seasonal ritual to do with the kids. We had a Nature Table (really a windowsill in the dining room) where we left leaves and flowers or rocks. Fairy things. To bring Nature inside.

And I totally forgot about the soup.

It had completely boiled over. An entire family-sized can of Campbell's tomato coated the entire range top I had totally taken apart and scrubbed with steel wool and soap and hot water just that very morning.

Sigh. I almost cried.

When Tamara came over that weekend, she'd just heard from our friend Julian that he'd done it. He'd served Tamara's husband the divorce papers.

She sat on my bed, her back against the wall, and covered her eyes. No tears, but overstimulation. Exhaustion.

I brought her a cupcake with a glowing candle in it to celebrate. She laughed and blew it out.

Later, she called to talk to her children who were with their dad. She cried then. When she heard their voices.

CHAPTER 24

lost ring

Losing my engagement ring before we got married always felt like a bad omen to me. I hoped I was misinterpreting the signs.

It had either ended up in a soccer field or in the trash can at McCornack Elementary School after washing my hands. I didn't even have a picture. My memory of it had faded. I was still so wretchedly disappointed about it.

My mother's wedding set reminded me of it a little, but it felt weird to wear my mom's set on my wedding finger.

I felt melancholy and depressed. I longed for sleep to blot out the numbness and, conversely, the ache. I didn't like how I felt. Sad in a scary way, like that ominous feeling that something bad was going to happen.

I'm scared.

CHAPTER 25
love and writing

The truth was, I wanted to feel alive with love and romance. I wanted to feel *in love*. In love with passion and thinking and yearning. I wanted to ache with longing for Paul. Instead, I kissed him and walked to my bedroom alone. He stayed up to play in his online world. I was afraid we wouldn't ever have anything to talk about—that our interests would change and we'd slide apart even more. We'd had sex only once that month—maybe twice.

I knew Paul was stressed and depressed about his daughter, ex-wife, and work. How could I give him space, though, when doing so seemed to create a chasm between us?

I wished I could paint my madness. My despair, my sadness. Reds and purples. Bruises on the heart. Paint it out. Painting seduced me with color and the potential ability to say something without words, when words were so scarce.

But writing would have to do. It was the only way to make sense of my world.

myself

I am a rose blush with teal sparks,
A curvy goddess
Who swirls and bops to a jazzy ballad in a smoky room.

I am the number 18, full of beginnings,
A roll-top desk with hidden compartments
Living in a sunset
In a sultry, mountainous forest.

I am a deciduous tree
Shedding fear
Each year
With passionate acceptance
Hidden behind my eyes.

A curious conundrum,
I let go of nothing
And everything.

I've forgotten how to forgive myself,
But I remember that
My soul is old
And knows all the answers to
My questions.

CHAPTER 26
first date

A year and a new couple's therapist later, I brought up an open marriage again. I just wasn't happy.

Paul and I put up profiles on a dating site called OkCupid.com.

I actually hadn't planned to. Paul put his up first. I wasn't actively looking for someone to date. I just now had permission from Paul to date someone I felt connected to, if somebody came along.

Paul put up his profile and tried engaging with women, but more than once, they accused him of cheating on me. He let every interested party know he was married and had an agreement with his wife about dating other woman. But nobody believed him.

Poor guy. I supposed he was only trying to get a date so that if I went out with someone else, maybe it wouldn't hurt so bad. It would feel worse if I were on a date without him, and he stayed home without a romantic interest to keep him distracted.

Looking back with the benefit of a decade to think it through, I wished I'd had the courage to just leave. In my mind, a "legit" way to get unmet needs met was to be with more than one man. I spent another year with Paul in therapy—part of that time in an open marriage, exploring polyamory (having multiple romantic relationships), convinced that this was a newly unearthed portion of my personality I'd never acknowledged before.

But I wasn't polyamorous. Not now, a decade later. Not then.

I should've left him years earlier.

To quiet the OkCupid suspicions, Paul and I decided I would put up a profile, too. That way, he could link to me from his profile to prove to the women he talked to that I was there and also dating.

I put up a profile and quickly got sucked into looking around. It was vaguely addictive, much like Facebook.

I found an Indian man I was interested in. Probably because he was from India. He sounded intriguing, so we started chatting and then made plans to meet at a local venue for a drink and an introduction.

I told Paul I had a date.

His response was noncommittal, and I told myself he wasn't interested in anything I was doing anymore. (*Lie.*)

Our plan was for Paul to stay with the kids after work while I went out with Nazim. My friend Brittany was having a birthday party that evening, as well. I'd go there after I was done with my meet and greet.

Tamara was planning to attend Brittany's birthday party with me, and as a precaution, Tamara was meeting me where Nazim and I were meeting at, just in case I felt uncomfortable or I needed an out quickly.

Paul called to let me know he was stuck at work, but wouldn't be too late. I briefly wondered if he was late on purpose, but felt evil for thinking it. I understood the absurdity of my husband hurrying home so I wouldn't be *too late* for my date with another man.

I started to feel chokey in my throat, like I felt before crying, so I held my breath and thought of something else. I readied the kids for bed until Paul got home. We awkwardly passed each other at the front door. I don't remember if I kissed him hello.

I walked into Cozmic Pizza on 8th and Charnelton and spotted Nazim right away. He was the only Indian man there. He wore a gray peacoat and black plastic-framed glasses and at one of the tall bistro tables, reading a newspaper. His eyes flickered up as I walked toward him. Nerd style, he stood up and pushed his glasses up his nose with one finger.

I smiled at the geekiness of it. Somehow, it made him more attractive to me. Don't ask me why.

He smiled, and we shook hands and sat down. We chatted and when Tamara walked in, we made eye contact. She continued past me into the main room and sat down at a table.

Nazim was charming, with a laugh that inhaled rather than exhaled. His teeth were white against his brown skin. He talked of India and his family. Asked questions about mine. He was curious about the open marriage.

"I've never dated anyone who was married," he said. "And your husband is okay with it?"

"Sure. Of course." (*Lie.*) "He's on OkCupid, too," I said.

I was equally fascinated with the person sitting in front of me, so unlike anyone I'd met before, and with myself. *Who was this person casually having a date with another man?* I stopped myself from shaking my head.

I breathed deeply and felt fully engaged, intensely interested in having this experience, and artfully stuffed any contrary feelings of guilt or betrayal. Paul was okay with it.

(*Lie.*) And I deserved to have some fun, to have a man's attention, to be flattered and made to laugh.

I didn't want Tamara to sit by herself, and I actually thought she would enjoy sitting down with us and continuing the conversation. I told Nazim about her, and he laughed. He said it was okay to invite her to join us, so I waved her over.

She smiled and cooed and flirted with Nazim just as much as I did, and the three of us had a funny conversation about knitting.

"It's so weird that you knit," Nazim said.

"Why?" Tamara said.

"It's something a grandmother would do."

"Not anymore," I said. "It's trendy. Lots of people do it now. Young people. It's not just for grandmas anymore."

Nazim smiled and shook his head, chuckling.

The three of us had so much fun together that we extended the conversation to Brittany's party. We didn't think she'd mind if we brought Nazim along. And I was right. Brittany smiled and raised her eyebrows at me when I walked in with him.

When I got home, Paul wanted to know how the date went. I told him everything. It was part of our deal, although I felt uncomfortable revealing to Paul how exciting it was for me to be with another man. I could feel myself blushing, thinking about it. Thinking about Nazim. I so loved all things Indian. I even worked the lunch shift at an Indian restaurant so I could wear the clothes, listen to the music, and eat the food. What luck that I was now dating an Indian man.

CHAPTER 27

nazim

I stumbled through my days—parenting, reading about polyamory, going to couples counseling, seeing Nazim for coffee dates and visits on the weekend while Paul was at work and the kids were with a babysitter. Then Nazim lost his job.

"Oh no," Paul said, with genuine worry, when I told him.

A global recession was not a good time to lose a job, especially for an Indian man without a green card.

It was such a weird feeling to be actively dating one man and married to another, with his sort-of, quasi-consent. Even though I knew Paul's consent was only verbal and didn't extend to his heart, I rationalized it wasn't my fault if it hurt him. It was his fault for agreeing to something he didn't want to happen. So I was in the clear. (*Lie.*)

When I thought of Nazim and the things I wanted to do with him, there was an unspoken agreement to never tell him what those things were. Because I knew it would make it harder for us to be together. So I imagined them. And this became the precursor to the fantasy life I would then have with Nazim for the next two years.

What I wanted to do with Nazim were regular, domestically intimate things. That's what I dreamed about. That's what I imagined. That's what I wished for. Probably because I didn't even really get *that* at home. And that's what I didn't tell Nazim about because I knew those domestic-y things would never happen for us either, and it just seemed to highlight our unique circumstances in a negative light. Made me fall out of the fantasy.

I wanted to visit India with him to see the places he missed. To eat his favorite foods. I wanted to drink coffee with him in the mornings. I wanted to leave things around his apartment for him to find. I wanted to snuggle up next to him before we climbed out of bed in the mornings. I wanted to share traditions and rituals with him. To hold hands while we shopped for groceries, to watch him shave, to shower with him. I wanted to kiss him every day, welcoming him home after work. I wanted to learn his native language from him. I wanted to drink chai on a Saturday and then bicycle to the Saturday Market together.

I wanted to know what parts of his tradition and culture he still instinctively did and the ones he did because he loved them. Which parts of his culture had he shunned or just didn't take part in because they didn't ring true for him?

Like, did he consider it not cool to eat with his left hand? In his family, was it rude for the wife to say her husband's name out loud? Were there any Hindu traditions that his family did out of respect for his mother's heritage? (She had converted to Islam to marry his father.)

I wanted to know if being one of the Muslim minority in India ever made him feel Less Than as he grew up. He'd spent some time in Africa as a child, but I couldn't remember how old he was while there. I wanted to know that too.

I wanted to know everything about him.

And I wanted to know what losing his job would mean for us because we were definitely Us by then.

CHAPTER 28

stuck in hypocrisy

It was a midmorning Sunday the following spring. Paul was at work. The kids watched videos in the living room. Time to write. Maybe it would turn into a personal essay, but right then, I just needed to empty myself. I headed into my studio.

When we bought the house, we intended to have Paul's mom live with us. My office would be her room whenever that happened. Probably the builder thought of it as a library or an old-fashioned sitting room.

Upon entering the house, my office/studio lay immediately to the right through French doors. Large windows looked out to the garden and the street, and the windowsill held candles and ceramics. A massage table set up for practice took up most of the room. We had hoped I could make money as a massage therapist, but that hadn't worked so well while unschooling a seven-year-old too old for daycare. My desk and computer were in a corner. Mara Freedman chakra prints on the wall reminded me to center and ground myself, and a deliciously filled-up bookcase—one my mother and grandfather built together—felt safe somehow.

That day, I felt raw and broken and weird and not very coherent. I felt trapped and stuck and I couldn't breathe. At an impasse, a stalemate, a conundrum of days and ways of life. And Humphrey had just eaten one of my shoes.

A brand new one, too. The only time in my life I'd ever bought a $90 pair of shoes.

I felt like I was grieving. *That's* what it was. Grieving for what? My body deflated with a giant sigh. I didn't want to spell it out loud on the page. I didn't want it to exist. But then I wanted it to exist. I wanted to act on it, and then I *didn't* want to act on it. I wanted to live a different life, but I wanted and cherished the very one I had. I wanted *less* chaos in my life because of the pull on my time and energy, and then I wanted to add *more* for the excitement and promise. I wanted to live authentically, with my true self showing at all times, but then I was too afraid.

Dogs, chickens, husbands, fantasy boyfriends—fantasy *husbands*, come to think of it—children, IEPs, homeschooling, gardens, special needs, doctors, therapy, traveling, writing, agents, editors, proposals, desires, and unmet needs.

I struggled with extremes. Paul once told me I had diametrically opposed dreams. (*Truth.*) Like, the fierce dream to travel around the world and wade in multiple cultures and breathe in their essences and write about them—*and* to live with a minimal footprint, on a mountain farm and ranch with a creek and tons of trees, living totally off the grid and completely self-sustaining.

But, I couldn't do both.

Who would take care of my animals while we traveled? Who would tend the gardens? How could I knit and sew all of our clothes and household items and still have time to write the books milling around inside me like lost travelers? How could I live my dream of using little to no fossil fuels and still fly around the world?

I would be (and was) the biggest hypocrite of all. (*Truth*.)

So, I sat in my office—with the compact fluorescent light beaming on me, and the dogs play-growling down the hall, and the kids yelling 'Don't bark!' and my son locking a dog in with me so they could hear their television show, and him scratching at the door so I had to get up and let him out so he didn't tear the paper blinds—and felt stuck.

Was I a bitch, opening my fingers wide to let loyalty and devotion slip through? Was I a bitch, welcoming my desire for other men and strutting in long skirts with mirrors and spaghetti straps and push-up tank tops? And walking with lengthy strides and swishy hips in *fuckme* boots and painted lips and eyeliner under Vogue librarian glasses?

Was *that* real?

If I closed my fingers tight and let loyalty and love pool in my hands—held fast—would I preserve my peace? Would I be accepted? Would I be honored? Did I have to shush the Me that lingered in trepidation, hovering over a panic attack of instability? Would I last?

Would I be real *then*?

Was I a bitch, selfish and singular, or was I real? Or was I both? Could I be both? Did I have to be a bitch to be real?

Could I live with my fingers closed and still be real?

I promised to be true to myself, to figure out the answer to this, and I vowed I would say my fears aloud until they meant nothing anymore.

In retrospect, while I deeply loved Paul, I wasn't *in love* with him anymore. Though I needed things from him I wasn't getting, I didn't have the courage to leave. (*Truth*.)

I put my fingers on the keyboard, even while the feeling of life was stuck in my throat. The only way to breathe was to write. Write so hard I could outrun the ankle-biting demons—the ones that taunted me with who I wanted to be and how different that was from who I lived.

CHAPTER 29

haunted

Nazim kept making sounds like he would move, but I held out hope that he wouldn't. I was definitely falling for him. He couldn't leave. If he did, I'd only have Paul, and the hole would be unbearable.

I didn't want to go back to feeling so alone. We had a good thing going, I thought. Whenever Paul was at work, I'd get a babysitter for a couple of hours and have a lovely date with Nazim.

Nazim couldn't stay in Oregon unless he found a job that would offer to sponsor him with a work visa. But what if he couldn't get one? What if they deported him?

He asked me. He did. He asked me to come to India with him. I would live like a queen, he said. He'd take care of me and cook for me and make me tea every day. He wanted me. He loved me. It killed him to see me with Paul, he said.

I wanted to go with him, to follow him. But I couldn't leave the kids. I couldn't leave Paul. We cried together, Nazim and I. He didn't want to go. He didn't want to leave me behind. He said so.

I felt upside down. Hanging. Shaking at my frame. What had become of me? Nothing smelled the same; I was haunted.

CHAPTER 30

why i wrote

I wrote to quiet the demons, the pesky ants that bit me and tickled my skin with their feet.

I wrote to capture dreams, to recall faces and emotions and what ifs.

I wrote to know myself.

I wrote to explore.

Myself.

And the world around me. But mostly myself.

When I wrote, I felt luxurious. Like I had all the time in the world. Like I was important and what I was saying was so important, I had to drop everything to write those specific words down or they'd be lost. Which, ironically, was true.

When I wrote, I felt like my words could make a difference in someone's life but ... it didn't have to. My actions could do that, too. Yesterday, I had friends over. I actually interacted little with my guests, yet I provided the space for them to connect and relax and feel safe. And THAT made a difference to them.

When I wrote, I saw birds taking flight, as Plato said, "to the world that is invisible and is sure of bliss." Promises, echoes, memories, callings. I saw imaginary animals and dreams and thoughts barely constructed. I saw the past and the future, but rarely the present.

I needed to remind myself to see the present because that was where all the parallels were. That was where the meat of it was. *That* was where I should write from. From the present. Write what I saw in front of me. That was what would help people.

And myself.

When I wrote, I discovered who I was. Whom I was meant to be. I discovered forgotten dreams. I discovered stories in the leaves and heard whispers in the foliage. When I wrote, I discovered charm and grace and wit that I didn't have in my speaking world.

That was why I loved to write.

Writing enabled me to access that graceful and creative place that wasn't so apparent to me otherwise. To reclaim all of me. To remember stories of other lives. Other meanings to things. A new perspective.

CHAPTER 31

spiraling

A few weeks later, I fought the hermit-ing. The drawing-in. And went to a coffee shop. I felt like a closed fist. White knuckled. I was conversely lonely and wanting to be alone. Nazim was moving to New Jersey. His sister lived there. He would stay with her until he found a job.

I didn't want the chai in front of me or the cold bowl of rice and chard. I didn't want to be at The Wandering Goat. I wanted to be asleep at home, but I had less than an hour until my shift at the Indian restaurant.

Paul was at work, and the kids were back in proper school—no more homeschooling. Paul and I thought it would help our relationship if we had more alone time together.

Nazim called me "my Queen." He washed my hair and my feet and looked into my soul with eyes that burned through my flesh and dripped into me like molasses.

He curved his skinny legs around mine and cupped his fingers around my ass, lingering, and bit me. His energy sank into my aura when we hugged, and he rubbed his face into mine when I cried.

When we spent time together, his scent changed, mingled with mine, reacted to mine. He said he couldn't live without me, that we had to figure out how to live and love long distance, so our love could stay passionate and real and fulfilling. Then he would trip in the dark hole of giving up and say he feared he'd never see me again.

"I think we should travel to India every year—go to a new state each time. No matter who we're with," I said once, before he left.

He nodded and held my hand.

Sometimes I thought about having another baby. Nazim's baby.

CHAPTER 32
how i was like my parents

My love life wasn't my mother's fault, but I witnessed her stay with my dad no matter what, *for years.*

There were so many times during our marriage when I should have left Paul. But I waited, loyal, not wanting to make waves, not wanting to hurt him, not wanting to disturb my children's lives with their new father. When my mom and dad got divorced, after I was well into my 20s, my mom had asked me if their divorce had disturbed me. Was I hurt in any way?

"No. I think you probably should've gotten divorced ten years earlier," I said.

Mom nodded her head.

My parents never seemed to have much in common. He smoked; she didn't. She was religious; he wasn't. They both treated money differently. They spent their evenings differently and separately.

When I looked at their relationship, I could see Paul and me. Like her, I stayed in my relationship longer than I should have, too.

My dad came from a class of people that stayed with the same job until they retired. There was no such thing as "I hate my job. I'm going to quit and find a new one." He was tenacious, too.

My parents showed me how to live my life. In some ways, unintentionally, I've modeled myself after them.

The things I did that were from my mom:

- Talk about housecleaning a lot.
- Think about housecleaning a lot.
- Make lists a lot (sometimes about housecleaning).
- Get up before anyone else, with a hot beverage.
- Not clean the house until it was way beyond even a brigade of Merry Maids before suddenly doing it all in one whole day.
- Stay with a husband for too long, because that's what you did. Plus, it would hurt too many people if you left.
- Realize one day that neither one of you were happy, so if you could not be happy together, then it would be better to be happy apart.

Things I did that were from my dad:

- Soldier on.
- Laugh it off.
- Outwardly portray a *Whatever, Go with the Flow* attitude and mask what was going on inside.
- Get pissy sometimes when things don't go your way.
- Feel mildly self-righteous every once in a while.

CHAPTER 33

leaving paul

On a spring day in April 2011, Paul and I talked at our dining room table. The kids were at school and it was a day off for Paul.

"This open marriage isn't working for me," Paul said.

"What do you mean?" I plastered on a fake smile, knowing exactly what he meant.

He didn't enjoy sharing me, but I dreaded what it would mean if he put a kibosh on it. Would I have to face my unhappiness yet again? Would I have to go back to the way I was before—lonely, neglected, and uninspired? Because that sounded horrible. (*Truth.*)

Not only would I not feel loved, but—and I was just understanding this—I was only a step away from loving Nazim. Maybe I already was in love with him. Only I hadn't given myself permission to do so.

With Nazim, I felt the strongest connection I'd had with a man since ten years before, when Rob died. If I went with Nazim and left Paul, I could have more children. Paul didn't want any more, but maybe that was too much of a convenient excuse.

I could also continue living polyamorously. Nazim accepted that about me.

But what if this swarm of emotions was just *new relationship energy*? I could lose family and friends over this. Anna, Paul's mom, could reject me, and I really loved her.

It would affect the kids if I left Paul. My decision would take the kids away from their dad—at least part-time—and their dad away from the kids. That's if everything went smoothly, and we agreed on 50/50 parenting time.

With Paul, I'd made nine years of memories. Some were not-so-good, but some *were* good—our Caribbean cruise, our Mexican honeymoon, our trip to Maui, buying land in Costa Rica so we could retire there, our hand-fasting ceremony along the McKenzie River, raising our children together, and all of those anniversaries.

Nine years of loving each other. Nine years of history, communicating, easiness, goofiness, laughter. Two children together.

But staying with Paul meant living a lie. Living monogamously. Pretending a commitment I didn't feel. Losing my romance with Nazim.

And that terrified me.

"I want to be with someone who wants only me," Paul said that spring day in the dining room. "You have to choose. Nazim or me."

"That's the beauty of polyamory," I said glibly, with the fake smile still in place. Maybe if I treated this light-heartedly, it wouldn't feel so wretchedly important. On the cusp of a seismic shift. "I don't have to choose." (*Lie.*)

"Well, I'm not polyamorous," he said.

"But I am." I gave him a gentle smile. (*Lie?*)

But looking back, I acknowledge my smile wasn't compassionate or gentle. It was condescending. Like a newly converted zealot, I truly believed that polyamory was an enlightened way of life because there was no way one person could fill all the needs of another.

People needed many, many others to attain happiness and fill the multiple needs of individuals, right? We already sought outside our family for some of those things. We drove to a farm to get raw milk; we went to a doctor when we were ill; we talked to our best friends about our problems. Paul and I didn't turn to each other for any of that. How was love any different?

True, I was getting love from Paul, but somehow I didn't feel it anymore. When I was married to Rob, I felt his love for me exude out of his pores. It washed over me and it buoyed me when I was near him.

Paul's love was a desperate love. It hinted at intimacy and closeness and, while he always urged me to explore hobbies and dreams, I didn't feel supported at home—with housework, the kids, or shared future dreams. His love felt needy—not suffocating, but paralyzing, in a bland sort of way. Lethargic.

Nazim's love felt free and safe and highly sexual.

Was Paul truly giving me an ultimatum?

YES. IT TURNED OUT HE WAS. PAUL CALLED FOR THE ultimatum: choose between monogamy with Paul or polyamory without him.

I swore I would never leave Paul. Gave my word. I never thought there would ever be a need, but I guess I meant there would never be a need to leave him as long as I had the freedom to grow. In this case, having the freedom to grow meant living and exploring a polyamorous lifestyle to see if it was really me.

But Paul wasn't polyamorous, and he was tired because he loved me. For me, he had tried to be polyamorous. He'd sacrificed over a year of his life, of our marriage, to see if he could be something he was not, and I felt shitty about that. I really did. (*Truth.*)

Nazim asked if Paul deserved to be given one more chance. One more honest effort at being monogamous with him.

Of course, he deserved that.

But I didn't know if I had the fortitude for that.

I still can't remember how the conversation at the table ended, or when the next one started, but I remembered crying in our bedroom together.

We sat on the bed, Paul nearer the pillows and I at the foot of the bed. We faced each other.

"I want a separation," I said. All my pores opened at once and heat flashed through every single one, instantly bathing me in an all-over body perspiration.

I looked down at the blanket and then forced myself to look at his kind and cute face, the face I had loved for nine years, at the man who had adopted my fatherless children. The man I had laughed with and kissed and fucked.

If I had to choose between Paul and Nazim, I needed some separation to see if I truly wanted to be away from Paul, or just thought I did.

We cried together and clung to each other.

When I looked back on this moment months later, I chastised myself again.

He said once to me, "You got whatever you wanted. I didn't want chickens. You got them anyway. You wanted to homeschool the kids. I didn't. You did it anyway. I feel like you've talked me into my life and I didn't want it that way."

At one time, I felt guilty about that, like I'd bullied him into getting my way. But really, if you spend years escaping from your life, you don't get to be devastated when it's not there anymore.

When I asked for a divorce at a later time, Paul insisted I hadn't given the separation enough time. But I knew I'd already said goodbye in that bedroom. It wasn't mine anymore. The bedroom or the marriage.

CHAPTER 34

no toes in the water

Moving out was hard.
I backed the U-Haul truck into the driveway and opened the rolling door, ramp out. With our garage door open, I brought furniture and boxes out to the U-Haul. I'd only packed my books and clothes and a few household items. Nazim said that he would leave his stuff with me when he moved to New Jersey, so I didn't need to bring a lot of things from what was now Paul's house, not mine.

Nazim hadn't found a job yet, but to save money, he was moving to his sister's place in New Jersey.

Months later, I thought to ask him, "Why didn't you stay with me and look for work here?" I never understood why he left in the first place.

"I don't know," he'd said.

Maybe he didn't know at the time, but his response should've put me on my guard, should've warned me of the things to come.

In true guilty fashion, I kept things that only I would miss. I took the silverware that Paul didn't like. I left all the CDs with him. I was going to take the goddess flags only I loved, but he said that he liked them now and wanted me to leave them. I agreed, of course.

My lawyer said later, when I refused to ask for spousal support or child-support in the divorce, that the lea*ver* always felt guilty and didn't want to take anything from the lea*vee*, but it was really okay—the right thing to do, in fact—to ask for child support. Paul made more money than I did, had a college degree, and had workforce experience, much more than I had since I'd stayed home to raise the children. It was okay to get child support. But still I said no.

Some things I really wanted but didn't have room for in my apartment. Like the wooden, handmade chest that my brother-in-law's father had constructed before he died. I had purchased it to put Rob's things in. I didn't feel like a Rubbermaid tote would be honorable enough to store his belongings in.

Later, when I moved into a house and had the room, Paul wouldn't give me anything.

But that day, as I loaded things into the U-Haul, Paul helped me. It was both devastatingly sad and pathetic.

"Will you still come with me when I have my surgery?" Paul held his breath, his lips pressed together. He was considering a medical procedure for an arteriovenous malformation he had.

"Of course," I said. I touched his arm.

Paul let a sob escape. His shoulders hunched forward. He grasped his own hands and sniffed.

I felt like an asshole, witnessing his gratitude. What kind of woman leaves her husband like this?

"I always felt like a loyal partner and wife," I said to my counselor in her downtown Eugene office after I'd moved out. "But how can I be if I'm doing this?"

Despite thinking of myself as loyal, the divorce struck me as completely non-loyal. The dichotomy of that warring faction scraped against my psyche like a rasp. How could I be both loyal and non-loyal at once?

"You don't see yourself as loyal?" my counselor said, "Because I do. You stayed in this relationship for nine years trying to make it work. If that's not loyalty, I don't know what is."

"Oh. Maybe I am then." Relief swished through me. Not enough to cancel out all my guilt, but enough for me to breathe that day. Whenever I felt like an asshole in the days that followed, I remembered what she said and repeated five words to myself like a mantra of acceptance.

I tried for nine years.

PAUL AND I TRIED VALIANTLY TO PREVENT OUR DIVORCE from becoming messy or drawn out, though we struggled with visitation rights and our parenting plan, which we needed to file with the courts. We almost went to mediation because we seemed to hit a brick wall at one point. Somehow, we stumbled through it with only mild animosity.

As the divorce proceedings began, I felt nostalgic for Costa Rica. We had bought land there together and had been planning a move with the kids in just a few short years. Three, in fact.

I missed planning for it and emailing the neighbors and talking to Paul about whether we wanted a driveway or where to put the laundry room in the Costa Rica house. And now I would not get to go.

And that was my choice. No one else made it for me. I totally acknowledged that. But it still stunk.

Months later, I still didn't miss Paul. I didn't miss sex with him; I didn't miss sleeping next to him; and I didn't miss spending time with him. I missed my hot tub.

Call me a bitch, but my muscles were so achy I woke up in a whiny mood almost every day. It was pathetic, really.

Also, it was awkward being around Paul—I didn't crave being around that.

Also awkward? Going to the No Shame Eugene Theatre show among friends I used to have who smiled and hugged me when they saw me, but had lost touch with me because of the divorce.

I saw a woman in a hijab in the audience and thought of Nazim in New Jersey.

I saw art.

I heard "I Am" in a powerful song.

I heard whispers and quiet footfalls and the warm chords of an acoustic guitar. My favorite. Struggling not to cry, I applauded instead.

I felt stupid in the skirt and tights I'd worn that night, and wished instead I could've hidden in jeans and the wool cap Tamara crocheted for me.

No hiding for me that night, though. I jumped into the fire; no toes in the water. In an effort toward normalcy, I decided to perform a monologue. I rubbed my fingertips together before walking on the stage, and my heart beat fiercely.

CHAPTER 35
writing about divorce

Divorce was for trying new things, like wearing fishnet stockings and dying my hair. It was for figuring out what was best for my children and maintaining my sanity at the same time. It was for starting new relationships and stopping them.

I'd been on several dates since Nazim left for New Jersey. One guy was promising. Jake was a giggly, muscular, triathlete artist. He wore his hair long in a ponytail and kissed exceedingly well. Totally my jam.

I was afraid to write anymore. Afraid of "friends" scoffing when I wrote about my bad/lonely/worried/nostalgic days, saying, "It's *your* fault if you are. What did you expect to happen? You shouldn't have left him."

Despite my fear and loathing, I wrote about what was happening and what went on for me. Writing was how I processed. Writing was how I breathed. Writing was how I showed up in the world. If I didn't write, then I wasn't really there. So, I had to break through the barrier. If people in my community didn't like what they saw on my social media feeds, then I invited them not to read it. They could always unfriend me on Facebook. Some did.

What helped me blog, even when I was afraid I was being melodramatic or self-indulgent, was remembering that, just maybe, I was helping someone else along the way, someone else going through a divorce. At least I could entertain them in some strange/sick/lovely way.

Writing about my divorce was tricky, though. There was always the censor dude in my mind with a taser gun threatening to zap me if I got too snarky, got too whiny, got too personal, said something that my ex would be embarrassed about, said something that would hurt my ex, said something that would alienate my friends—our mutual ones anyway—or said anything that made me look bad.

I knew a writer who wrote about her divorce for all to see, with no censorship. It was awesome. So refreshing, so real, so honest. And so damn funny! I wanted to do that. Write without censorship. And. You know. Be funny about it.

CHAPTER 36
jake dates

Jake met me at my Lincoln Street apartment on a late spring afternoon and we walked to the Kiva to get some groceries. He talked about his family, giggled at himself, and parkoured off buildings while we walked. Maybe he had nervous energy? He carried my box of groceries home while I shared my own stories and struggles.

It was so different not having the kids around all the time. In some ways, I could breathe finally. Could think thoughts without interruption. Could heal. Could *feel* without them watching. But I also wanted every spare minute with them and felt full of rage that Paul got an extra night with them. It would've been so much better for the kids, especially Robert and his difficulties with transitions, to have a week-on, week-off schedule. But no. Paul wanted to always have them on his days off, regardless of how it impacted the children.

In the apartment, I put away the groceries and offered to make Jake a chai. He opted out, but took a glass of water. He didn't like hot drinks.

I resisted the involuntary shudder. Once a beverage was of

gulp-able temperature, it was too cold for me. I hated ice, and sometimes even warmed up water in the microwave to drink it.

While my chai heated on the stove, I moved closer to Jake. He was about my height. Maybe an inch taller. That meant our lips were perfectly aligned. I moved into seduction mode, and he giggled again. I wrapped my arms around his shoulders and played with his ponytail. His lips were full and warm.

I put on some music and we lounged on the living room floor, talking about movies and our lives.

"I want to take this relationship, or whatever it'll be, slow. If that's okay with you," Jake said.

"Sure." I smiled.

Nazim and I video called almost every day, but I hated the long distance. Dating Jake was fun. I enjoyed being with him. It didn't matter to me how fast we did anything.

We took turns sharing songs we liked. My favorite at the time was Deb Talan's *Whetstones*. His was something by Katie Perry.

At some point, we both felt comfortable enough to move closer to each other on the floor. Jake sat with his back against the love seat Nazim had given me. I had been keeping space between us out of Jake's request for a slow start, but as he got closer, I followed his lead.

He reached his hand out and traced my arm up to my shoulder. I scooted closer to him and rested my ear against his collar. He turned his face toward mine and I closed the gap completely.

A couple of minutes later, I sat up and stretched.

"What happened to wanting a slow start?" I asked.

His kitty-cat smile matched my own, and he shrugged.

"I don't know," he said.

He stayed the night.

CHAPTER 37
jake and nazim

I wiped down tables, cleaned the buffet, seated customers, and buzzed through the lunch rush. The noon rush was just slowing down enough for me to catch my breath when, out of the corner of my eye, I saw someone new walk in with a rolling suitcase. I knew who the guy was. I always had to seat him somewhere where the suitcase wouldn't trip people. He wouldn't leave it at the coat rack. Probably a student.

I came around the bend to get a pitcher of water so that I could seat him. I looked up. It wasn't the student.

It was Nazim.

Standing there. Right in front of me. My breath stilled. He was here. In Oregon.

"What are you doing here?"

"Surprise!" Nazim grinned broadly.

My eyes flitted over his torso and jeans and smooth hands with buffed fingernails. I drank him in, catching at all the little drops at the bottom of my need, still greedy for more. I hugged him fiercely. I pressed my face into his collar. He smelled of CK cologne, and I stifled a groan.

Three days early. He'd surprised me. The romance of it didn't escape me. I wanted to kiss him. Instead, I gave him my keys.

He picked me up after my shift. His brown fingers curled around the steering wheel as he carefully pulled out onto Franklin Boulevard.

"How long are you staying?" Somehow he'd never arranged that part. I just knew he was showing up this weekend. He didn't have a job to go back to yet, so the return date was left up in the air. But I figured he must've bought a round-trip ticket. So when was he actually leaving? How many days did I get with him?

"Forever."

I froze. Blood in my body that had ceased pumping when he left months ago once again began flowing. Parts of me that had been dead, thawed. I drew in a ragged breath and filled my lungs with oxygen. Tears started in my eyes.

"Really?" I sobbed, relief wracking through my shoulders. I gripped the armrest and then pressed my fingers to my lips, stifling my cries.

"Val." He looked from me back to the road. "No. I can't stay. You know that. But I wish that were the answer, I wish that were true, that I could stay forever."

"Why would you say that?" My voice scraped over the words, freely crying.

He stammered and stopped. His attempt at levity and flirting had failed miserably and only hurt me. I could see in his face that he understood that, too.

The beginning of our time together was ruined. For the rest of his trip, we stroked each other and kissed and made love and he cooked for me and we had long conversations and went on walks together. It was lovely but tainted with a sick disappointment that permeated everything we touched or said to each other.

It was a shitty thing to do to me. I don't know why he left in the first place. To save money? We could've lived together while he looked for work over here. Why did he have to move all the way across the country to look for work? We could have had more time together. But no.

I never understood why things happened that way. Except that maybe it was supposed to happen that way.

The universe has ways of teaching us things. And if we aren't ready to learn them, they just come back into our lives over and over until we get it. Until we evolve.

On our last morning together, Nazim made me tea while I remained in bed. He rattled around in the kitchen. It sounded as though he even put away my dishes from the dishwasher. We'd talked so much that long weekend I didn't even know what we'd talked about. Everything. My eyes roamed the ceiling and traced the orange peel pattern. *He will leave today.*

As I lay there feeling shriveled up—nothing left, dried—but also raw and oozing, Jake texted me. My heart pulsed, once. Like a spike on an EKG machine. I'd been dating Jake since I divorced Paul, and Nazim moved away. It was weird to text with Jake while Nazim was in the kitchen. I felt conflicted.

Before, when I was married to Paul, any other romantic or sexual interests I had were easy to keep separate in my head. Compartmentalized. And each relationship fed me in a way that the other didn't.

With Nazim and Jake, the commonalities blurred and crossed over a lot and, honestly, I found it a bit more difficult to segregate them in my mind. I would grab Nazim's shoulder blade and remember that Jake sometimes called that a Buddha Hold. I'd be with Jake, romping around on the floor, and he'd sniff my armpit.

I'd flash to a time when I'd been with Nazim, because he did that all the time. When Nazim held my hand after the movie yesterday, during our walk home from the theater, I pictured Jake and I holding hands on a walk, searching for chocolate, the week prior.

They both looked me in the eye when they talked to me or for no reason at all. They both touched my skin just because. They both loved my imperfect body because it was that way. Which wasn't bad. It just wasn't what I was used to, and managing those two relationships differed from what I had expected. (*Truth*.)

I answered Jake's text and went to take a shower.

After my shower, Nazim and I sat in the living room on the couch, drinking the tea he had made for me. I always melted a little when Nazim handed me a cup of tea that he'd made for me. He always cooked it on the stovetop, with actual tea leaves, adding cardamon, milk, and sugar. The attention to detail endeared him to me.

We smiled at each other and blew on our tea. The silence was comforting.

"I have to tell you something," he said. "While you were in the shower, I read your journal."

"What?" My skin cooled and my body stiffened. I set down the mug on the coffee table and stood up. Backed away. I didn't remember doing that, but I can see it now, as I write this.

"It was lying just there and I couldn't help it." He stood, too.

"You read my journal?" I shot laser beams with my eyes. I felt them leaving my eyeballs, and I hoped he felt the singe on his skin. Revulsion raised the hair on my arms. "That was *private*," I said. What a shitty thing to do. Unethical. Fucking creepy is what it was.

"But what I saw made me happy," he said. He moved to the other side of the coffee table and put his chai on the bar. He faced me. Attentive.

"Like what?" I said.

I had been writing about Jake. Even though Nazim and I were not exclusive, my emotions and time with Jake were still private. I shared some things about our tentative relationship with Nazim, mostly because he found it strangely sexy. He liked me telling him about when I was with other men.

"The part about how you think you've found a good match with Jake."

I glared at him, but I sat down again. Cross-legged. Made myself smaller. I didn't notice that until now, either.

"It makes me happy to know that you are taken care of here." He gestured with his hand and leaned back against the bar. "I'm not here to help you when you need help. I'm glad that you can get your needs met with someone else."

He meant sex, of course. It sounded logical, though. As a Virgo, Nazim was always logical. And I was grateful that he was open to not being exclusive. I loved him, and I was fairly certain he loved me. He told me as much. But I was starting to have feelings for Jake, too.

Being polyamorous meant that I could love more than one person at a time, and I felt like I was getting close to that. That I was letting my heart get involved with Jake. And I knew for certain that Jake reciprocated my feelings. I really liked Jake.

But that confused me, too, and frankly, it hurt, too. I was heartsick a lot in those days.

Nazim watched me. Waiting. But I didn't know what to say to him. I pressed my lips together, indenting the underside with my teeth. Biting. But not biting. I took a sip of my chai again, so I wouldn't have to speak.

Why couldn't he just stay in Eugene?

Maybe the concept of polyamory made more sense in theory than in practice. Logistically, it was hard to share head and heart space with two men. I had no problem loving them both, but the day-to-day part was confusing. Did each man get their own days of the week?

Paul had said during our marriage that he would only feel a loss with me dating someone besides him if he felt neglected. For instance, if he was home and I was out on a date, that would feel bad. Or if I was with him but clearly thinking of the other person, that would hurt Paul, too. So when I dated Nazim while still with Paul, I always made sure to be with Nazim when Paul was not home.

With Jake and Nazim, things were both easier and more complicated at the same time. Because Nazim was not local, I spent my time with Jake. And the more time I spent with Jake, the more my thoughts drifted from Nazim to Jake. And I really liked Jake. I closed my eyes and tried to separate my feelings between the two. But Nazim was still watching me.

I wished Nazim could just stay in Eugene. That would solve everything. I would choose him in a heartbeat, but he wasn't here. He was leaving today. Leaving me again.

"Why can't you just stay here with me? You can look for work here."

"I can't."

"Why?"

He joined me on the couch, and I leaned into him. He didn't answer me.

On bad days, I couldn't stand the distance. And Jake was here. And I needed the companionship. Here. Every day. Not once every few months.

But.

I swallowed down a rush of confusion.

Did that mean I wasn't polyamorous?

My heart hurt. And that made me angry.

I wasn't usually prone to anger, but it rose in wispy currents up my legs and tickled my spine until it burned my throat. And all I could focus on was the invasion of my privacy.

I sat up and pulled away from him. I clamped my molars down until they ached.

I pretended our conversation was over. That I didn't need to share my feelings and concerns about him and Jake. About me and Jake. I gulped at my chai as a distraction, but it had gone cold.

Reading my journal was *wrong*. I didn't care if what he read *was okay with him*.

CHAPTER 38

robert vs. nazim

I pulled up alongside the Village School cafeteria's side door and trotted in to pick up Robert from After School Care. He always hated leaving his friends and the toys and games, but my restaurant shift ended a mere forty-five minutes after the school day ended.

Sometimes I let him stay longer, just for fun. Today had been one of those days. Nazim was still visiting, and I wanted as much alone time with him as possible.

In the van, Nazim came up in conversation.

From the back seat, Robert kicked the bucket seat in front of him. Thankfully, not mine.

I glanced in the rearview mirror.

"I don't like it that Nazim sleeps in your bed." His fingers fisted in a tight squeeze. "It feels like you're trying to replace Dad, and the only time you can do that is if he dies. And Dad's not dead!"

I sighed, my eyes back on the road. I'd read about parents that let their kids veto any of their potential partners, but I was not one of them. I didn't like the idea of Robert or Clover not liking Nazim, but it really wasn't up to them who I dated. On the other hand, there had been so much change in the kids' lives with the divorce, I hated upsetting them any more than was necessary.

Was *this* necessary? Nazim? My kids were more important to me than Nazim, or I'd be living in New Jersey already. I rubbed my hands one at a time on my shalwar pants, but the steering wheel stayed sweaty. What could I say to Robert that would be supportive of his feelings and stress, but firm with my own boundaries?

"Of course he's not dead. But I'm divorced from him. I'm not married to him anymore. I don't believe the same way you do. And that's okay. We don't have to."

Robert glowered the rest of the way home.

NAZIM HELPED ME WITH LAUNDRY ON THE LAST DAY OF his visit. He was going to catch a shuttle that would drive him to the airport, so that I wouldn't miss a work shift.

We folded the clothes coming out of the dryer and stacked them in the laundry basket. So many things left unsaid.

I watched his profile as he concentrated on making tight, professional folds. I folded haphazardly, not caring about wrinkles. My kids didn't even care if they had folded clothes, or even if they were in a dresser. Sifting through a laundry basket was fine with them.

I didn't know what to say that I hadn't already said or alluded to. *Don't go. Why won't you stay with me? I love you; doesn't that mean anything? If we got married, we wouldn't have to be apart.*

I didn't even bother thinking of the things I didn't—*couldn't*—think of yet.

Why should I bother then? I don't think I can wait for you to get a green card. Love shouldn't be this hard.

We finished the laundry, making small talk that was ridiculously painful and pointless. Painful *because* of its pointlessness. We were just killing time until I needed to take him to the shuttle and get back to pretending my heart wasn't broken again. (*Lie.*)

On our way to the shuttle, we stopped at a café for one last outing to add to our memory banks. We took pictures of us together and of each other, greedily, so we'd have something to return to.

Because of Nazim's extreme privacy, he prohibited me from posting pictures of him on the internet. His family didn't know about me—he'd told his sister he was flying to Eugene for a job interview. Potential employers searched the internet for what applicants got up to in their social life, and pictures posted on the internet stayed there forever, he said.

I grudgingly agreed; it was his right, his face in the interwebs. But as I solemnly—and with a dose of irritation—cropped him out of all the pictures I posted on Facebook, I felt ever more distant from him. How could he want me in his life but keep me a secret? And why did he get to decide that I could *say* I had a boyfriend, but that no one could see him? Did that mean there was no proof of his existence? And if there was no proof that he was really there, and that most times he *wasn't* really there, then why was I waiting for that? Why was I crying over that? Why was I agonizing over that?

Later, after Nazim had left and Robert and I were taking a walk by ourselves, he brought up the divorce again.

"Why did you divorce Dad?"

I never knew what to say to questions like that. I always struggled with how much to say, what was developmentally appropriate for a child, and how much honesty was safest for a nine-year-old kid on the spectrum.

"Because I didn't love him anymore." I decided on blunt honesty, but simplified. Robert always appreciated direct communication. His autism didn't allow for the nuances of beating around the bush.

He scuffed his feet and bent down to the sidewalk, dislodging a leaf stuck to the ground.

"I'm afraid you'll stop loving me, too. And leave me, too," he said to the concrete.

I almost choked on the sorrow in my throat.

"No, baby." I kneeled down and held his hand. "I'll never stop loving you. Never ever."

"But you stopped loving Dad."

"Yes, but you're different. You are a part of me. You lived inside me before you were born." I hugged him. *Part of you is still inside me. We share the same DNA, the same blood.*

Did I say that? Or think it? I can't remember.

He held my hand, and we continued walking.

"But Dad is part of you. He's still inside you. Because you had sex."

I didn't stumble. I didn't gasp. And I didn't laugh. But all of those things flashed before me. Sex education was a good thing, and I was glad his school promoted knowledge on that topic.

"Well," I said. "It doesn't work quite like that. There is no part of Dad still in me. But you are." I squeezed his hand.

CHAPTER 39
foreshadow

Nazim and I Skyped almost daily. But, our communication changed. It became tiring. He was always asking me to have logical reasons for why I did things. Why did I make plans to see Jake without asking Nazim if it was okay with him? Why did I think it was a good idea to have Jake around my kids?

He wanted to analyze my decisions. Nazim was my boyfriend and had the right to ask me about any manner of things (*Lie*), but I just didn't do things that way. I based my decisions on a feeling and went with it. If things didn't work out, I jumped in a different direction until things started working and it felt right.

When I talked to Jake, there wasn't a lot of explaining. We talked with a similar lingo, and that was comfortable. We'd watched the same cartoons as kids and had listened to the same bands. We had similar spiritual and artistic backgrounds, too. And that excited and filled me. It inspired me to think, act, and create more around him.

As the Skype sessions became longer and longer, Nazim wanted more attention from me, and I felt mildly panicked.

I didn't want to put a lot of effort and heart into a long-distance relationship. Plus, he'd found a job in New Jersey, and it sounded permanent.

There was always a hope that Nazim would get far enough into the green card process that he could quit his job, find work back over here, and not have to start over with the immigration paperwork. Since I loved Nazim, of course I wanted to wait it out and see if he could come back.

But he was jealous, and that raised my hackles. He insisted it wasn't jealousy, but what else was it if Nazim didn't want to share me with someone else?

I talked with Tamara multiple times about this. She liked Nazim, then didn't like him, then liked him, and disliked him again.

I think she liked him just fine, but when I was unhappy, she hated him. Said he wasn't good for me. Sometimes I listened to her and calculated ways to break up with Nazim. I really hated the long distance. And things were good with Jake. Very good, in fact.

I really, really enjoyed spending time with him. Our bodies fit together nicely, and I liked the way he giggled. He was soulful and creative and silly. I almost loved him. But loving two men at the same time had proved complicated, so I was careful about letting myself get that far this time.

At least, not until I had my head on straight. Because it was occurring to me, I wasn't as polyamorous as I had once thought.

And that was alarming.

Once again, I was in a relationship with a man that I loved but wasn't getting my needs met, but I didn't want to leave him because I was loyal, *dammit*. I didn't want to be the person who flitted from vacation sex to vacation sex. From man to man. From job to job.

And I felt like I owed something to Nazim. He had sparked something in me, awakened me, despite the cliché, and had given me courage. Courage to leave Paul and the nine-year relationship that wasn't working. I would always be grateful to Nazim for that. (*Truth*.)

I thought Nazim had made me courageous, that I was stronger when I was with him. But underneath, I knew that wasn't true. Though I couldn't let that truth come to the surface yet.

I felt like a lonely zombie, wandering the streets, not understanding, having no direction, no meaning. It hurt to be apart from Nazim. I was willing to wait for him (*Lie*); I just didn't know how to do that.

I found myself standing in the shower, staring at nothing, not even remembering I was in there. I acted as if I was grieving or in shock, but I wasn't. Just heartsick.

I actually did that a lot. That staring.

It wasn't very productive.

CHAPTER 40

possessiveness

My son, in his new loft bed, murmured in his sleep. I bought the bed because Clover wouldn't let him do "sleepovers" on the new bunk beds in Clover's room, and I felt bad for him. So we had a used Craigslist loft bed delivered. He was pretty stoked.

At the restaurant, I again requested a weekend day off, and my boss finally agreed. I now had a whole weekend day with the kids. When the weather was nice, we could go to Saturday Market or play frisbee in the park.

I wanted life to be more normal for my kids. The divorce was hard on them. I tried to make the changes more exciting, rather than terrifying.

I laid on my mattress on the floor because it wasn't the right size for my bed frame. I followed the lines on the ceiling and wished I could paint the rented walls. Imbue life where there wasn't any. I wished I could paint myself.

Robert moved in his sleep, the metal frame of the loft bed swaying.

I felt sick to my stomach. Empty, hopeless, numb. Nazim

wasn't crazy about sharing me with other men, but he understood my polyamorous needs. If we were married in the future, he insisted that any side relationship that I had outside of him would have to be kept secret. No one else could know that I had other relationships. It would be scandalous to his family and bring shame to them.

So my polyamory would have to be kept secret—my identity, my personality—from his family and from our mutual friends.

I used to think I wanted to be in a relationship with Nazim, seeing men on the side. I had waited for it. Strived for it. But, again, I wasn't on the same page with Nazim, and we were thinking of two different things. Two different outcomes. We didn't see eye to eye about any other men in my life, if they ever happened.

According to Nazim, these other men could never be my boyfriends. There could never be a strong emotional or spiritual bond with them.

And that made me sad. Like a piece of me was being told to sit in a closet in shame. Surely that couldn't be what Nazim wanted for me. I needed to touch him and smell him and reassure myself that we'd always be in love with each other and always in each other's lives, no matter what that love looked like.

I couldn't hide myself. I didn't like secrets—to be one or to have one. It was too much of an emotional burden to bear.

I couldn't even withhold Christmas presents if I bought them too early. I literally couldn't wait and sometimes bought a second present to cover up that I'd already given the recipient their actual Christmas present.

The secrecy was toxic to me. Hiding a piece of my personality was harmful, yet Nazim said his parents and sisters mustn't know I even existed right now.

I liked truth and honesty and authenticity.

Maybe this didn't have to do with polyamory at all. Maybe it didn't even have to do with relationships. Maybe it was about Nazim needing control and guarantees in his life and wanting assurances of how things were going to turn out.

I understood that desire. I got that. But it was also one I'd already processed for the most part. I'd come to terms with never having control of the future. I didn't even know what the future could look like, and I'd gathered a bit of skill and mental flexibility along the way. I knew I'd be okay with whatever life brought me because I could show up and live and deal with and accept whatever happened. Things happened for a reason. I was curious enough to find out why.

Sure. Sometimes my life was hard, and it threw me for a loop. Maybe I'd spend thirty-six hours in a numb stupor or three weeks not eating enough or not cleaning my apartment, but I would figure out why it was happening or not and adjust. I'd make it work until I found happiness. (*Still a lie though.*)

I didn't think Nazim had reached that level of maturity yet. I saw a lot of red flags there.

Whenever he felt frustrated with me, my thought process, or my actions, he had an unfortunate habit of exclaiming, "Are you naïve?" It hurt my feelings.

He talked a lot about being angry. I had seen no huge outbursts, so he either processed his anger well or stuffed it down, and I was afraid of what it'd look like when it blew up.

More and more frequently, he seemed to act out of a sense of what *he* called entitlement (*Like that was somehow a good thing?*), but it looked more like *possessiveness* to me.

The previous night, on a Skype call, he told me he deserved a monogamous relationship, despite a short, non-inventive fling every once in a while. I cried.

"Why are you crying? I'm not mad. We're just learning

about each other and we're still in this relationship. We're still trying to make it work," he said.

But I was thrown back into Paul's dilemma of poly versus mono. If I stayed with Nazim, I might have a glorious life, but there would always be a bit of inauthenticity. There'd be an unexplored part of me left to atrophy. And that scared me.

All my life, I had followed a set of rules and expectations without thinking for myself. I really wanted to do that for myself now. I wanted to explore what it was I wanted my life to look like, not what I thought was best for others or hiding for fear of rejection.

Sometimes, I already felt married to Nazim and felt a nurturing sense of a softer, selfless way of devoting to him, because he'd given so much of himself to me. I wanted to reciprocate, to show gratitude.

Who was to say that a sacrifice like would go unrewarded? I would find love and joy in my relationship with Nazim. I knew it. (*Lie.*)

Perhaps that would be enough. Maybe I wouldn't feel drawn to other men. Maybe I'd be able to stay more neutral about those crushes and stop seeing them if they started interfering with my life with Nazim. (*Lie.*)

Maybe I was worrying about nothing. (*Lie.*)

"I don't want my life to be an experiment," Nazim had said.

But it so totally was one. How could life not be an experiment?

"I want to be damn well sure that who I give my life and soul to will do the same for me," he said.

Which totally sounded like Paul. Almost *verbatim*. Red flags galore.

I steeled myself and sat up in bed. *Dammit.* I would just love Nazim so much that I'd be willing to give up that part of me. I'd love him so much I wouldn't ever look at another man.

I'd love him so much, none of this other stuff would matter. (*Lie. Lie. Lie.*)

In the bathroom, I brushed my teeth with force.

A nice sentiment. But was it realistic? Was it sustainable?

No.

I spit and set my toothbrush down.

CHAPTER 41
fear tingles

Tingles and fear got mixed up sometimes. Tingles didn't *have* to mean fear. They could mean that feeling I got when I'd had two and a half glasses of wine and my tongue didn't move quite as well as it used to twenty minutes ago, but it still thrilled me. Or tingles could mean that someone I loved was tracing his fingertips along the skin of my back. Those tingles were good.

And then there were the tingles that weren't good but still didn't equal fear. Like when I bumped my elbow on a doorjamb.

But today I felt the tingles that equaled fear. The ones that started at the base of my skull and shot neuro-tendrils, like Medusa snakes, up around my entire head. Now, I had a helmet of tingles, and the hairs on my arms stood up ... maybe to see what was coming next.

I shrunk smaller and backed into something—a corner, a couch—for protection and looked around me, smelling the air. Was something there? Had someone got into the house? I had heard nothing—no window rattling open, no breathing. But still

I felt it. The tingles spanned my whole body, and I breathed faster and tried to hold it at the same time—just so I could hear better. Hear whatever was coming.

But nothing was.

There was nothing there.

I went and checked four times. The closets and curtains. Under the beds. I checked the locks on the windows and the three at the front door. Nothing.

There was nothing there.

Then what was it?

What made me feel that way?

Why was I afraid?

There was no *rational* explanation. My mind wasn't playing tricks on me. The neighbors weren't making any noise. So, I moved on to the irrational explanations. Had it been a ghost? Was it Matrix déjà vu?

I closed my eyes and imagined myself with my Mind's Eye, going within, swishing through black tunnels to some unknown but vastly important destination. I strained to keep up and felt the connection slipping, so I breathed into it again. Relaxing, I swished off down the tunnels again.

And there it was. Around that last corner.

That thing.

I stopped and choked. When I saw what I saw, a horrible knowing swam up to me and when I acknowledged it, I opened my eyes to the living room. But it was too late. The knowing was already inside me, poisoning me with blackness and fear.

Could I do anything to prevent what I saw? Would there even be time?

The tingles subsided and my breathing returned to normal, but I looked every room over before entering it for the rest of the day and I couldn't help but feel uneasy. The knowing lingered and seeped out of my pores, like garlic did the following morning after I ate it.

I ignored it, of course–the knowing–and went about my daily routine. It had nothing to do with me. (*Lie.*) It would probably never happen again.

But it *had* happened. And had happened years before, with Paul.

Those tingles
that equaled fear
and started at the base of my skull.

The first time I felt them, I knew, but I lied to myself until I forgot those tingles. Now they were back, and I knew what they meant.

I needed to break it off with Nazim.

I wouldn't be happy in a long-distance relationship. I knew this about myself.

CHAPTER 42

first attempt

It was a Dear John letter, but I tried to be compassionate and grateful. Truthfully, those were the emotions I had then.

I told him how much I loved him and how much all the memories we had were so important to me, but that I just didn't have the strength to be in our relationship anymore.

I drew a shaky breath after that. Relieved. Free. Sad, *but whole*.

The next day, Nazim called me.

"I was at work when I got the email," he said.

"I printed it out and took it to the bathroom so I could read it again. I sat in a stall and cried, Valerie. I *cried*. I was a zombie the whole day."

His voice was flat. Tinny. "At home, I looked so ill that my brother-in-law offered me marijuana." He chuckled, but it was hollow and rasping. "I don't know. Maybe he thought it would make me feel better."

"Did you do some?"

"No," he said, accusing.

I said nothing. I guess I knew he'd have something to say about me breaking up with him. It was hard to keep strong, not to cave in like I did with Paul that time in the bathroom when I promised I wouldn't bring up an open marriage again.

Funny that I thought of that just then.

"I was going to tell my parents about you this year. Tell them I'd found The One."

My heart thrilled at that statement, but a little niggling part of me also thought, *Too little, too late.* And, *Why bring that up now?* I almost didn't believe him. Maybe a part of me even didn't. It was also shitty timing and like a slap in the face. "I'll tell my family about you" was a gross reminder that I was a dirty little secret, and *that* felt shittier than any of it.

Why would I go back to that?

We spent hours on Skype. I cried through most of it. Nazim looked like he was going to throw up through most of it. I felt like a complete shit.

I didn't want to hurt Nazim. But I didn't want to hurt myself either.

Should I stay with him? Was this the one I was supposed to be with?

What if he was, and I didn't stick it out? What if the green card process only took a year, and all I had to do to wait for my true love was to give it *one year?* I'd given more than that before to other men. It was a sacrifice to be sure, but wasn't it a worthy one?

In the end, he convinced me to give it an *honest try.*

"You haven't given us a chance. Not a real one," Nazim said. "Not if you're dating other men. Why don't we try to make this an exclusive relationship? Why don't we give it an honest, real try? And if it doesn't work, then we'll know. But how can you know if you don't try?"

The crying exhausted me. Trying to figure this out

exhausted me. I was exhausted from making a decision, and then being talked into something I wasn't sure I wanted, and then feeling guilty, and then, and then, and then.

Even though I felt shitty doing it and coerced, I agreed to an exclusive relationship with Nazim. Just like I did with Paul. But I was too exhausted to remember that then.

I wrote another letter. This one to Jake, to whom I'd been getting closer and closer.

He was also hurt.

It was supremely crappy timing for us, too. I'd gone to his house the day before and consummated our relationship in his space for the first time. We'd only ever had sex at my place before yesterday. It was a new level of commitment and acceptance for him. And I was dumping him the very next day. I hated myself. (*Truth.*)

Jake and I emailed a couple more times back and forth. Attempting closure, I think. I really liked him as a person, too. We had a lot in common. We had fun together. Why *couldn't* we be friends? He was fantastic with my autistic son, as well. I wanted him to be a part of my life. A part of my kids' lives.

Jake and I decided on about three weeks of not seeing each other at all, and then a tentative wandering back into doing friendly social things together, like going hiking or having coffee together at a public restaurant.

I talked to Tamara the next day in her kitchen.

"I'm so mad at him," she said, referring to Nazim.

Actually, she was livid. She stomped around the kitchen, slamming cupboard doors and smacking dishes around the sink.

"This isn't about picking between Jake and Nazim, Val. *It's about not being compatible with Nazim.* You're not good together."

"I don't agree," I said.

"You're in denial," she said.

I looked away, the dining room chair suddenly uncomfortable.

I also conveyed my "re-entry" plans with Jake to Nazim. He was less sure that a friendship with Jake could work, knowing me. I secretly agreed, but wasn't willing to relinquish a friendship with Jake just because Nazim was jealous.

"I'm not jealous!" he said.

I still didn't believe him. Nazim was a jealous man.

But he was also proud of me, and I sucked that up like I was dying of thirst.

"I'm proud of you for being honest, even if it was scary," he said. "And one day, if it gets too hard and you need to break up for real this time, I'll still respect you for trying."

I hoped that day would never come. It was too hard to do again.

CHAPTER 43
of bangles and bhangra

I threw myself into my now monogamous long-distance relationship that I'd never wanted. I had to have the right mindset. That was all. (*Lie.*)

I watched Hindi movies like crazy for ten days straight. One almost every night. I started going to a *Bhangra* dance class. I listened to Urdu music on my iPod. And I was reading—wait for it—five books on Islam, India, religion in India, a Pakistani/Muslim memoir, and a novel set in India.

Those were the things I did to ease my separation pain, to make me feel closer to Nazim.

Also, talking to him every day on Skype, *still*. Multiple times, really. I'd Skype with him when I got off work, and then we'd take a break while he ate dinner, and then we'd do it again. Sometimes we cried together. Other times we laughed and whispered love-y things to each other. We talked about culture, and we talked about our unmet needs and how much we missed each other.

We texted, too. And talked on the phone.

Both of us looked for jobs for him in the Pacific Northwest.

As a manufacturing engineer, Nazim couldn't take just any job. He needed to find a job that fit his schooling for his visa to be extended. And find an employer that would invest thousands of dollars in the visa/green card process. But it could still happen. (*Lie.*)

We dreamed about the future, while trying valiantly to stay in the now—taking one challenge at a time.

Some days I felt strong, others weak. But every day I loved him more and more. And that's what I held on to. That was what I'd go to bed with at night. Any night. A Tuesday night, say.

Just another Tuesday night.

How many more Tuesday nights would I spend without him?

I'm thinking of sex
And sweaty foreheads
And whispered conversations.

I'm thinking of soft
Squishy couches
That have seen more
Action than most.

I'm thinking of attar
And incense

Of bangles and Bhangra
Of Portland
And dancing
And moving slow.

*I'm thinking of laughter and Bollywood
Of Cat Powers
And werewolves*

Of Islam and punk rock

Of coming close to your fire.

*I'm thinking of high-speed bike rides in the night
Of kisses
And sleeping shoulders*

*Of his skin
And his smell.*

CHAPTER 44

again

I was staring at the wall again.

It felt like a boulder was pressing on my lungs again.

I was in that place where I couldn't breathe. Where I couldn't think. Where I could only mourn.

Whatever that meant.

I was in that place, again, where all I wanted to do was sleep. Where all I wanted to do was watch movies to escape.

Again.

Where I wanted to touch myself to forget.

Where I wanted to touch myself to remember.

Again.

I was in that place again where sleep often mocked me, unless I was falling asleep on the keyboard.

Where I floated through my life's existence like a ghost, watching from above.

I wanted to crawl under a mossy log and hide from drippy wet rain that seeped into the knees of my jeans and matted my hair.

It was that time again where I had to breathe fast and

shallow to get enough air because my lungs had so much weight on them, I couldn't wiggle out from under it.

It was that time again when the alarm was ringing and I couldn't find the off switch.

It was that time again where I turned the crank on the popcorn maker, and nothing popped. I just turned and turned and turned. And I thought of how that was a pretty crummy metaphor for my life, but a breeze forced its way past the blinds and lifted my hair, cooling me.

And tickled my calves.

And I smiled in spite of myself.

CHAPTER 45

journaling

One night, after a long sabbatical from journal writing, I propped myself up in bed with a blank book and a green pencil emblazoned with soccer balls. I rolled my eyes.

Do other writers succumb to this?

Lying in bed with a headache and flannel pajama pants, writing just to be writing something? Anything? Even if it's drivel?

There was a *Firefly* episode where Mal was rescuing River from a crowd of townspeople attempting to burn her at the stake. With Mal's gun pointed at them, they said, "But she's a witch!" And Mal said, "Yeah. But she's our witch."

Drivel?

Yeah. Well, *it's my drivel. And at least I'm writing it.*

I was finding more and more that when I was reading someone else's blog entry or someone else's essay or someone else's memoir, I abruptly stopped in mid-sentence, huffed, and found my pen—intent on writing my own words instead of reading another's.

Writers read to study their craft, but not as a distraction from doing the writing. From doing the bleeding on the page. From doing the opening for all to see.

It was Nazim's birthday, and I wasn't with him. And it hurt so much.

Actually, it didn't *hurt*. It was different from that. It was hard. It was difficult to move my body. I felt old. Like I did when Rob died.

I thought of Jake. I wasn't Facebook friends with him anymore, but I lurked on his profile page enough to believe he was most likely seeing someone else. She worked at Clover's school. Maybe I'd even see him there someday when I picked up Clover. That would be weird.

I felt desperate and wondered if my desire to marry Nazim and have his baby was just the agony of being alone.

If he were living in Eugene or Portland, I wouldn't feel the need to marry him. Yet.

It would grow naturally, not because it was the only way I could see being with him now.

If I married him, he got a green card. He moved in with me and the kids and eventually found a job. We started a family. It seemed simple to me and I didn't understand why Nazim didn't see it. (*Lie.*)

My mind wandered all the time. Sometimes I stared out windows and at objects on my bookshelf without actually seeing anything.

I just wanted to sleep it all away.

I had dreamt the previous night that Nazim told me to comment on one of his mom's Facebook posts, by way of slowly becoming seen by her. And I was so happy that he was getting close to, and setting the stage for, introducing me to his mom.

I wondered if she knew about me yet.

CHAPTER 46

a black hole through another's eyes

When I saw myself through Nazim's eyes, I saw myself as a loser. I saw a scatterbrained, talks-big writer who didn't really do anything about it, sex goddess.

Through my friend Julian's eyes, a slightly infuriating yet lovable friend.

Through Tamara's, kin. A soul sister—affectionate, fun, safe.

Through Paul's, a disloyal beast.

Through Jake's, an inspiring artist drunk in love with words and silliness. Confident.

I've heard that we are attracted to persons who shine out the very quality we lack. Was I only thinking of Jake these days because he represented the creative spirit lying dormant beneath my skin? Was I frustrated with Nazim because I saw my disappointment in myself behind his eyes? He swore I did not disappoint him, so it must be mine that I saw.

We all held mirrors up for each other. So why did I see disappointment in the Nazim mirror, but magnificence in Jake's? Based on that, of course, I wanted to spend time with

Jake—as a friend, of course. Who wouldn't want to be reminded of their brilliance and turn away from not being good enough?

Or was this just a story I was telling myself?

Perhaps I should spend time really focusing on personal growth, building creative castles in my skies, and talking with people. Awakening after a winter of depression, being born anew, making pacts with myself. Rediscovering. Rediscovering what things had cost me to live inside. Seeking answers with Nazim. And not being ashamed. Welcoming people in to see the real me. Emboldened. Emblazoned. Creating art with no rules.

Letting all my words be true when I spoke them, especially to myself. Asking myself, "What is right and true at this moment?"

Would this *whatever* I had with Nazim contribute to my artistic calling? Or take me away from it? Would this action, direction, person, situation allow me to feel Spirit? And express Spirit in whatever manner called to me?

I wanted to be inspired by Nazim's art again, by his photographs. I wanted to feel madly in love with him again. (And that sounded like something I once said about Paul.) Because this distance had dulled all that for me.

I didn't know what the future held, but I had a sick feeling that my visit to New Jersey wouldn't rekindle what we once had in Eugene.

There and then, I made a pact—to be honest with myself, to be authentically me, to not censor myself *to me*.

CHAPTER 47

coming back into myself

I needed to re-evaluate what brought *me* back to *me*. When I was feeling discouraged or emotionally under the weather, what could I do to nurture myself?

Not enable myself to develop destructive habits, for one. Like eating cheese by the handful and staying awake until one-thirty in the morning, watching Netflix movies—which I'd been doing. Instead, really *nurture* myself. Like a slow ritual of lighting a candle and deep breathing and stretching out like a languid cat. Burning incense and reading.

Or finding joy in art again. Going to a museum. Visiting friends.

Journaling.

I loved journaling, but I'd been avoiding it lately. I definitely found myself when I journaled. But when I felt depressed and didn't want to look too closely at myself for fear of finding something I didn't want to own up to, journaling was hard.

All of my interactions with Paul seemed tinged with his spite. I didn't understand why, though. He had a lovely long-term friendship with his other ex. Why couldn't he even be civil with me?

I didn't hate Paul. I just didn't want to be married to him anymore. I didn't love him like that anymore.

I recently met up with my other thirty-seven-year-old girlfriends going through divorce—There were so many of us!—and we started talking about online dating. Two of us had met our ex-husbands and/or current boyfriends online, and two of us had met them through regular social means. And two of us were currently on an online dating site.

Online dating, the merits and demerits of it, would be a suitable topic to write about, and I had an idea for a new twist to my blog. Plus, online dating *was* something that a lot of women have had, or would have, some experience with. Also—and especially because—if you were a single *mom*, the chances of going through the online dating experience probably quadrupled or something. I mean, if you were a single parent of small children, were you going to go to a bar to pick up guys? Well, maybe you were, but that was beside the point. The point was, online dating was becoming more and more prevalent and less and less taboo.

So, when my lady friends came over, we pillaged through the snacks everyone had brought, made ourselves drinks, settled into the living room of my apartment, and started laughing immediately about nipple size, blogs and small children ... also marbles.I opened up the online dating topic. I wanted to know what attracted people to certain profile pages. What packed what one woman called *Oomph* or said, "*Oooo!* I wanna go out with *that* guy"?

What things were red flags for people looking through the ads?

"Clearly, if someone puts that they are looking for 'honesty and no drama,' they have issues with those things because those are just a given in any relationship," said one member of my Divorce Support Group.

I wanted to know how many messages to send to each other before meeting the guy. What was the right amount? Did they message back and forth for a month? (Something I'd done.) Or meet after only one message? (Something a friend had done.)

I also wanted to hear online dating horror stories, but I didn't get any. Instead, we talked for hours about how easy it was to get a boyfriend, if size really mattered, or if it was the "usefulness" of his (points down there)—"yes, and yes"—and confirmed that it's "girth overall" that does it. For some of us, anyway. Other topics: reasons for divorce, male role in society, penis preference, chemistry and whether it's instant, and how learning each other's grooves takes a while. Also, that "stiffy" had more than one definition.

"In anyone's experience," one woman asked, "have you ever had a time where you're not that attracted to him at first, but then somehow you find yourself really horny for them later?"

"Absolutely."

"Really? 'Cuz I've never ... "

(Laughter.)

"Well, sometimes there are maybe characteristics besides their face that ..."

(Laughter.)

It was a fabulous night full of connection with women and Divine Cupcakes, laughter, letting our hair down, and support. Lots of that. And while I didn't get the answers to my questions about dating across the generations, the merits of different dating sites over others, and what women are really looking for online, I got to talk about porn and community and the beauty of male anatomy.

CHAPTER 48
not meant to be alone

Every other day, I turned around and ran into a Jake memory. It seemed hardly fair because I'd only dated him for six weeks. Such a narrow window of time to accumulate memories, but there it was.

One night I was feeling lonesome, so I asked Julian to come over. We didn't write together anymore, but I seemed to call on him more and more for an anchor. A spiritual tether. He was my friend. My platonic brother. He stayed with me when I was lonely. He stayed with me when he was lonely. And we talked. We danced. We ate. We cooked for each other. And we took walks. We asked questions of each other and made observations about each other. And sometimes they were ... not what we wanted to hear. We'd tried fooling around once or twice, but it was too weird. Incestuous. He'd only ever be a *brotherfriend*.

That night, he held me and played with my hair for two hours. We fell asleep on the couch and woke up around two or three in the morning. We, half-asleep, moved to the bedroom.

The first hour on the couch I'd been like a sponge, soaking up all the human skin touch. Only then did I reciprocate. But when I touched his forearm, I felt Nazim's arm. When I draped my arm or leg over him, I felt Nazim's body under mine. It was unsettling. I felt disloyal and weak for wanting, *needing* touch from someone other than Nazim.

"No one should be alone," Julian said. "We aren't designed for it."

Irony of all ironies, or perhaps it was synchronicity, Julian told me out of the blue that Jake went to ecstatic dance, too. The same community that Julian raved about, that was his tribe, that he'd been recommending I attend.

I wonder if it's a sign.

I started going soon after, and it was the best thing I could remember doing for myself. Not because Jake was there. It had nothing to do with him and everything to do with me.

I walked to the WOW Hall on 8ᵀᴴ and Lincoln, mere blocks from my apartment. The weather was mild, but gray. The breeze lifted my hair. I opened and closed my fists and watched the cracks in the sidewalk—I still tried to step over them. I was terrified. I swallowed and wiped my lips, blinked back tears. I didn't want to cry in front of anyone. I didn't want to talk to anyone. I didn't want anyone to look at me.

I didn't know what to expect.

I didn't want to go.

But I'd promised Julian. He didn't make me promise, but I'd said I'd go and that was the same thing. Julian knew me. Knew my issues. My hang-ups. And he said it would be good for me to go, and I believed him. I really did. But I was still scared. Not scared, creeped-out. But weird inside. Like stage fright. Like, not breathing scared. Like, afraid of falling into myself and never coming out, stuck inside of myself. Trapped. Trapped, scared. Scared of myself. Scared of what I'd find inside if I looked.

When I did this type of excavating with words, I knew how to monitor the depth. Sometimes I'd write a phrase that triggered a memory or emotion that got me crying. But I could stop writing if my emotions got too uncomfortable. I could avoid myself with the dishes or running errands. But dancing? In front of people? Who wanted to interact?

What if I faced something I couldn't process in real time, in public?

I stopped across the street from the WOW Hall and looked both ways, but on a Sunday morning, on a not-too-busy street anyway, it was just a stalling technique. A few people talked out front on the steps. One walked from her car with a paper coffee cup in her hand. One man locked up his bicycle under the trees next to the building.

I took a deep breath, crossed the street, and walked up the stairs into the building. I kept my head down and refused eye contact.

Inside, several dozen people milled around—some stretching, some praying at an altar set up on the stage, some stowing coats and bags on the benches. Everyone took off their shoes. A circle of people started forming in the center of the room. Ambient music played from a laptop playlist hooked up to the venue's sound system. No one talked.

Mildly relieved, I sat on a bench and took off my shoes.

The playlist ended, and a facilitator called everyone to the circle. We held hands.

"Welcome to Coalescence, an ecstatic dance group. Any new people today?"

I reluctantly raised my hand. A couple of others did, too.

"Welcome. We like to think of ourselves as a container for movement. Express yourself with any movement you want.

There are a lot of bodies here today, though, so please be mindful as you move around so no one is hurt.

"This space is a no-speech zone. Please go out into the hall or lobby to talk. But if you feel called to make noise along with the music, you can. If you feel like dancing with someone, a good practice is to make eye contact first to see if the person is open to a dance partner. We don't want to touch someone without their consent. And, if you are approached and you don't feel it, maybe smile and dance away from them. It's pretty easy to tell when people are open to dancing together.

"There are several *house tenders* here today. So if anyone feels unsafe or uncomfortable or just has a question, you can always come to any of us."

A few of the people in the circle said hi and waved.

With clasped hands, the circle collectively raised their hands and let go at the top.

The man that lead the circle went to the laptop and started a new playlist. Folks drifted to all areas in the room as the music moved through a spectrum of slow to fast in all different genres. Some did yoga. Some laid on the floor. Some hung out at the altar. Some raged around the room. Some did ballet. Some danced together, rolling off each other, entwining.

I mostly swayed in the back, feeling out of place. But as the two-hour dance window progressed, I felt less scared and stiff. I moved my body. I cried. I closed my eyes and felt the music move in my veins, like blood.

CHAPTER 49
it's winter

I could tell it was winter again because my feet were cold. I was weepy, and I stood in the middle of the living room looking at the coffee table laden with books and magazines and candles with wax-less corners and blackened rims. Or I stared at the vitamins in the kitchen and wondered and fretted over if I should read or maybe write a letter to Nazim to apologize for my being over-emotional during our last chat session earlier that day—if I even *had been* over-emotional.

I knew it was winter because I was inside a lot. Not inside my apartment, but *inside*. Inside my brain, my heart, my fears, my hurt.

I knew it was winter because my throat was sore—and not because I had strep or tonsillitis—but because I was holding my breath. Holding myself in tight from the cold.

I knew it was winter because I looked for meaning in everything until my brain stem hurt and I got thirsty.

I felt haunted in the winter.

I was slower.

Less sure of myself.

Less positive.

In movies, when the two people get trapped behind a rockslide or cave-in and they're running out of oxygen—all sweaty, sleepy and scared—they breathed slow and shallow.

That was me.

In the winter.

When it was eight thirty at night and it was black outside and the wind whined and the leaves stuck to my shoes like leeches, it was winter.

CHAPTER 50

how to eat sweet paan

Nazim picked me up from the airport in Newark. He looked so normal, standing there. The same. Somehow, I thought I'd see something new about him because we hadn't seen each other for so long.

In the car, he kept looking over at me, saying, "I'm so glad you've come."

We walked down a sunny street in Edison, New Jersey, a small town heavily populated by a large Indian community. In fact, that's why we'd gone there. We were on a search for a *Diya* (oil lamp for altars and prayers), more s*alwar kameez* (Indian dresses with matching pants) for my waitressing job, and a shop to fix one of my silver-belled anklets. We also wanted *burfi* and bad. It was my new favorite sweet.

"You want to try some *paan*?" Nazim said.

"No!" *Eew.*

"Why not?" he laughed.

I wrinkled my nose and grimaced.

"Isn't that the stuff that's red and you spit it on the sidewalks all over India?"

He laughed. "Yes. But no. I don't want you to eat that kind. I'm talking about *sweet paan*. You want to try new experiences, right?"

And with that logic, we stepped into a sweet shop and made our purchases. Two boxes of *burfi,* a *sweet lassi* (a yummy yogurt drink), and—with trepidation—*sweet paan.*

Sweet (*Meetha*) paan was a betel leaf wrapped around coconut, rose paste, candy-coated fennel seeds, and ... other stuff. The idea was to stick the whole thing in your mouth at one time, bite into it, and hold it there while you suck out the juice. Bite and suck. Repeat.

It was really sticky. And it was too big to fit into my mouth all in one go. So, I bit it in half.

The taste exploded in my mouth. It was like eating incense. People traditionally ate *Meetha paan* after a big fancy meal, like at a wedding, for digestive but also for social reasons. Though you could eat them after any meal.

I enjoyed it. It made me feel more Indian, and if I could be more Indian for him, maybe Nazim would tell his family about me. Maybe I'd be enough for them. More palatable. Indian enough for their only son.

While in New Jersey, I cleaned his apartment, and we went to IKEA and bought a rug and a new couch for his living room. He took pictures of me and played me his favorite music. We had lots of catch-up sex and walked around the autumn-strewn neighborhood.

Nazim took me to New York, and we ate at restaurants, picked out the locals by the way they rode their bicycles through New York traffic, and explored the Metropolitan Museum of Art.

We held hands, and he rowed me across Central Park in a rented rowboat. We laughed and teased each other.

I took loads of pictures of him to remind myself he was real while we were apart. I cried the day I left, and he held me.

Dear Jake,
I'm writing to say I'm sorry.
That's all.
I'm sorry.

I'm sorry for the manner in which I broke things off with you. It felt wrong to disappear like that. Especially after promising you I wouldn't. Two strikes against my principles.

I've been feeling guilty about this for months. And I've felt guilty for feeling guilty—telling myself I did it for my relationship with Nazim and I shouldn't feel guilty for wanting stability in that.

But the bottom line is I acted in a way that goes against my nature, against what I think is right and true. And that hurts me. Continually.

I'm writing to put right that wrong.

Sometimes I feel ready to have that smoothie/cup of coffee with you. To grow a friendship, to talk about art.

Maybe we could write to each other awhile, ease into it.

I know hearts are resilient, but they also scar and stay raw for a long time.

Maybe not enough time has passed to build friendship without a tinge of regret or sadness.

But...
The truth is,
I'm sorry.

And I wonder about you. How you're doing. You and your pigtails and the blue skirt you wore the last time I saw you.

Respond, if you want.

If you can.

Find me on Facebook again if you like.

Namaste,
Valerie

CHAPTER 51
i get my dog back!

My dog Humphrey had spent the last six months since the divorce with Paul, who never wanted him in the first place, and who crated him while he worked ten to thirteen-hour shifts at his workaholic job. It was fucking dog abuse.

I got sweaty and sick to my stomach every time I thought about it. When I left Paul, after an exhaustive search through Eugene's classifieds, I found a place that took dogs. The dog-friendly house wouldn't have been ready for a few weeks, but Paul didn't want me in the house anymore—he couldn't even abide me sleeping on the couch. So, instead, I had to forego the only place that took the size and breed of dog I had, and slept at Nazim's until I found my apartment. Nazim had already given notice at his place, which didn't accept pets anyway.

The more Paul neglected Humphrey, the more distraught I became. Lamenting to Anna, his mom, one day months later, she startled me with a brilliant idea.

"Why don't you look for a new place? You have the time to look around now."

I was gobsmacked. Of course! Why didn't I think of that? And then my heart fell to my feet with the weight of a bowling ball. *Why didn't I think of that?* Poor Humphrey. My little love. I loved dogs like nothing else.

I visited Humphrey at Paul's sometimes. I was mad and disgusted at Paul for neglecting Humphrey, and I was mad and disgusted at myself for neglecting him. I was the one who left. I would *never* do that to a pet again. *Ever.* I signed that vow in blood and have kept true to it for the last decade and counting. So, I found a new place.

I'd felt great since spending time with Nazim in New Jersey—*It worked!*—and he said he'd try to get tickets to see me on Thanksgiving. I could plan to get out to New Jersey and visit him again in January. On really strong days, I thought I could last the days and months.

Whenever I heard the rain pattering outside my bedroom window, I thought of the aftermath of making love to Nazim, of our tangled bodies and stroking his sweaty back with my fingertips while we listened to the rain.

However, I faced moving again and, despite my recent time with Nazim, I was still lonely and now, the last Eugene memories of Nazim would be stripped away. Us walking from my apartment to various places downtown. Us in the very room where I stood. Him making me tea in my kitchen. Us sleeping on the couch, making love in different rooms. Doing laundry together.

I wanted this relationship to work so badly that I was telling myself it was just time—that was all. I could be patient. I'd just wait. (*Lie.*)

But...

But.

Waiting hurt.

And it was bad for my health. (*Truth.*)

By that point, I'd been in a relationship with Nazim for one year. Facing a one-year anniversary of a long-distance relationship that, most days, I didn't want to be in was sobering.

It wasn't comforting.

It wasn't sexually rewarding.

It was lonely.

And.

As with everything.

There was no guarantee for the future.

And that rankled more for me.

Time to head back to the page. My journal was where I figured stuff out. It was where I unwrinkled the crumpled thoughts and fears.

I couldn't wait to move into the new house, though. It'd be *six more weeks* before the prior tenants were all moved out.

"Whatever. You'll be packing. It's not that long," Tamara said.

Call me insane, but I didn't actually think I'd need to pack. It was just a few blocks away. Like fifteen or something. I thought I could make a few van trips with some laundry baskets full of clothes and kitchen utensils and it'd be done.

The house was in-between my two favorite areas of town, with flat ground for biking, and near-ish to the kids' schools. Not as near as they were from the apartment, but nearer than Paul's house.

It had a fenced back yard that came with a chicken coop, an electric fence around the coop area, a plum tree, raspberry canes, garden area, beautiful bamboo, and a shed that locked. So no more stolen bikes. Humphrey would be back! And I told the kids I'd get them a kitten.

It was a three-bedroom, one-bathroom house in West Eugene, all hardwood woods (swoon) and a large kitchen and—I was so giddy—a wood stove.

My new landlords were people I already knew and admired—Eugene Waldorf School parents and teachers—and their daughter was in Clover's class at school.

The previous tenants had painted all throughout the cozy cottage in different colors, not just Rental Ecru. And the house was one that I felt like I could really be alive in. Really be me in. The colors were a little off my personal color wheel but so close, it was ... well ... kind of weird actually, like seeing something through warped glass. They were the same colors I liked but different hues. The *Merlot* bedroom that would be mine wasn't the jeweled purple I preferred. It was more pinkish. The blue and turquoise bathroom was a *Skype* blue, rather than the royal blue on the Mexican tiles that I loved. And the dusty peach living room walls were more ... *Wendy's Special Sauce*.

Again, all the hues gravitated toward my colors but ... not quite the right shade. I didn't think I'd be painting over the walls anytime soon; the colors were too freakishly close, and that seemed important somehow.

The kids' bedrooms were not yet assigned. I mentioned the colors of the rooms to them. One was yellow and the other a reddish something that would be perfect if it had a bit more brown in it.

"Not yellow!" they both said. Fast. Like saying, "Not it!"

So. That room would have to be re-painted. Ironically, it was the only paint that came close to being the color hue and shade I would pick. I loved yellow. The paint was just a little *eensy* bit too bright, but it was so cheery, and it matched the navy bamboo printed curtains perfectly. Of all the rooms, it was the one I'd least like to paint over. Huh. Funny.

Probably, the yellow room would end up being Robert's. I didn't know why that was except that when I walked in, I just *felt* it was his room. When I tried to describe my hunch to him, he got all offended that I would pick his room out without him there. He didn't get it.

The only thing that slightly marred the perfection of the place (other than the strangely parallel-universe paint choices) was that the back door for Humphrey the Dog was in my bedroom. And I didn't like the idea of everyone traipsing through my bedroom sanctuary to go to the backyard.

But it didn't matter. Humphrey wouldn't be stuck in a fucking cage anymore.

CHAPTER 52
julian

I woke up to another overwhelmed morning, feeling so discouraged I wanted to bury myself in my bed, skip yoga class, and write. Skip Robert's school concert that neither my son nor I wanted to go to and make soothing lists and schedules instead. Those lists were usually the only way to calm my befuddled mind. That, or escaping into a movie, which was easier than escaping into a book—which, ironically, created more stress because there were so many books I wanted to read.

I needed to remember my grandfather's way. He did so many creative things. He grew dahlias and cacti, had a cactus business, made jewelry, polished stones in tumblers, did woodwork, and experimented with computers. Probably he did all that after he retired—now that I thought about it. Plus, he didn't do it all at the same time. He picked one immersive hobby at a time.

I couldn't do everything I wanted in my life all at once. Not even my grandpa could do that.

Even after one day, I loved my new space, especially since Humphrey lived with me now.

Julian texted me one night after I'd gone to bed, offering to stay with me any night I'd be alone, when the kids would be with Paul. It was good to hear. I was afraid to take him up on it, though.

What if I got attached to him?

Stupid. Of course I should get attached to him. He was my friend. I should let friends in close and lean on them. And who better to be affectionate with?

There was no miscommunication or mixed signals between Julian's actions and my own, because we both knew where we stood sexually and emotionally. It was a relief, and I knew that if I started getting lonely and missing a body to lean on, Julian could provide that for me. And that made me feel safe. But I knew that the type of snuggly touch I did with Julian would be really confusing to someone else. It looked like something it wasn't.

He really was like the gay friend I'd always wanted. Minus him being gay, of course, because he wasn't.

CHAPTER 53
dance metaphor

I walked up the stairs to the dance floor at the Vet's Club. Each step felt heavy and my knees already hurt, weighed down with depression and funk. I didn't feel like dancing that night. I felt like writing or crawling under wet leaves in a forest and smelling the loam of the earth in my nostrils.

Dance was the perfect metaphor for life. Sometimes, the music sucked; sometimes, the song ended before I was ready; and sometimes, it dragged on. Sometimes, I got smacked alongside the head, bumped, grabbed, or brushed against. And sometimes, I danced my boundaries wide and demanded my space.

Sometimes, I danced with my eyes closed and got testy or even tearful if someone invaded my space. (But I wasn't protecting it if my eyes were closed.)

Sometimes the song screamed for a partner even if there wasn't one for me. Sometimes the beats mirrored that of my blood, pulsing through my limbs, and I felt hope blossom as I connected to the larger, to the Everything. When that happened, I smiled, and love seeped out and touched my tribe. I belonged.

Other times, I didn't feel safe. I couldn't hold my space, and I retreated to a corner, resentful that I couldn't stand or dance or lie down where I wanted. Sometimes, I felt left out. Sometimes, I cried because, in dancing, I uncovered feelings or fears or truths.

Sometimes, I raged and fought the urge to give up and sit out of a dance, or to not show up at all. Most times I found a new way of expressing what was real in me, and I was breathless with the knowledge that I might've missed it.

Other times, it felt fine to honor the impulse to sit down. To look at something else. To experience the sounds and messages with a different medium, listening from afar instead of swirling in the middle of it.

Sometimes, I felt disjointed, and I didn't understand the meaning, the why, the purpose. The music set just didn't work for me.

I wanted to dance through life with my eyes closed because I could best hear the songs that way, could hear how they moved me. Hear their instructions for my soul. But people ran into me then, and I got hurt.

Dance was a perfect metaphor for life.

CHAPTER 54

cologne and a day off

I woke too early on my day off. My children were with Paul, so I was hoping for a good eight to ten hours, but was only granted six. Upon waking, a fearsome vision greeted me—the nightmares where I'm partially awake. I gained alertness as the vision increased in its horror, and by the climax, I was fully awake, though paralyzed from shock and sickness.

Awake in my bed, I tried to redirect the end of the nightmarish vision. I always had those violent visions when I felt out of control in my life.

But I *was* in control right now, I promised myself. (*Lie.*) I could stand the time apart from Nazim. (*Lie.*) It could be fulfilling. I knew it could.

I was in control. (*Lie.*)

The nightmarish *thing* threw me off kilter for the next hour and a half while I wrote in my journal in bed and soothed myself with all my loving memories of Nazim.

His brown hands, his heat, his passion, his voice, his love, his tenderness, his laugh—the real one, not the chuckle. The way his foot jiggled, the way he said vitamin (*vit-ah-min*), the way he danced, the ways he took care of me, his dreams that he was careful to keep inside himself now, the black hat he wore, the way he shared everything he had with me—his furniture, his advice, his milkshake, his money, his love. I felt safe with him.

I decided not to let any funk attach itself to me. It was just a dream, even though I was awake during most of it. It was just a dream. A nightmare.

I still struggled with shame from time to time regarding those *visions*. Strictly *because* they happened while I was awake, I felt like somehow I caused them. But that wasn't true. They only snuck up on me when I was feeling overwhelmed and out of control, weak, and they always had to do with some violent, horrible fear. It was always myself or someone I loved getting hurt or dying in the visions.

I also knew they weren't my fault—that I didn't cause them —because they started happening when I was so young. Thirteen. My son suffered from them now, too. Maybe from the divorce? Maybe from his anxiety-producing sensory processing disorder? He was ten, and he wasn't doing that to himself. He wasn't bringing it on himself. And *I* wasn't bringing it on myself.

I swallowed my thyroid pills and looked around my room at the little tokens of love Nazim had given me. A heart-shaped box. A gold fabric bag. His bed.

I stood in the kitchen with bare feet, and a black-and-white striped button-down shirt of Nazim's I often slept in. While I waited for the tea water to boil, I emptied the dishwasher.

After a sip of tea, I turned on my computer to see if I had any new messages in the last seven hours.

My bra and *kurti* lay discarded on the sofa. I smiled. Nazim said I was like a little child, taking my clothes off whenever and whenever I wanted.

A text from Nazim:

> Good morning, whachaupto.

> Reading blogs about writing, getting excited about the conference, and drinking tea.

I didn't tell him about the nightmare where we'd had a baby —a little girl—who died after birth.

I spent an hour surfing the internet, made more tea, ate a banana. Nazim called me on his lunch break, and we talked for about twenty minutes.

I spent way too much time on the internet (but it *was* my day off) and ran some errands—one of which was getting a wireless router from Goodwill.

When I got home, Nazim was waiting for me on Skype. We chatted and shared links and laughed about "You Americans and your sweets" while *he* was eating a cupcake. After we hung up from our video chat session, my landlord came by to tell of the parking lot resurfacing at a neighboring church that might cause traffic problems for me and fixed my wobbly doorknob.

I ate dinner and watched the Spanish film, *Plan B*. Then I paid bills. *Ugh*. Back to nothing again, and it was only the third of the month. Talk about living on the edge.

Then it was midnight. Time for me to brush my teeth and close my eyes. I was so tired that I didn't have that empty-bed sadness. Also. No funk. All Day.

I could do it! I could be in a long distance relationship.

Nazim made everything better.

Just his presence. Just him being alive.

And then. Just for a moment. I smelled him in the living room. Not his cologne scent, but *him*.

Maybe he was dreaming of me right then.

At 3:00 a.m.

In New Jersey.

CHAPTER 55
i might not sell my house for "just cool"

My shaman-in-training friend, Julian—my *brotherfriend*—and I talked one night about how to re-access Spirit through dream gates. Of how to talk to Soul again.

I was making roads, honoring my needs, letting go of old baggage.

I was learning ever more about myself.

I was slowing down.

I was looking at my experiences with more maturity and less obsession.

And.

Also.

I was trying to reconnect with my intuition.

Rob's death catapulted me into talking with him in the pages of my journal, of receiving visits from him in my dreams, of meeting my spirit guides and my soul family. Of trusting myself. Implicitly.

But not anymore.

None of that was true anymore.

My *brotherfriend* and I talked also about trusting myself again.

Well.

It wasn't really *distrust*, like I was afraid I'd steal my laptop from myself, but more like when I checked in on some uber-important question for soul and self, I wanted to know that the answer I received was coming from a place of wholeness, not from fear or desire.

Or co-dependancy.

Getting back to that place might take some time, and I was horribly out of practice. But I wanted to know that I could tell myself the truth.

All I knew to do was dance until the dream gates opened, write until I heard the clarity that didn't come from me, and dialogue with people who reminded me to check inside. *All the time.*

"Is this bringing me closer to my goals?"

"Is making this choice in line with my true calling?"

"Will I be proud of this decision?"

"Am I communicating in the most nonviolent way possible here?"

"Will chocolate *really* help today?"

"Is this me being authentic?"

Other than the general reasons of personal growth and authentically living a life I could be proud of, the reason I needed to know if I was lying to myself, or more accurately, that the answers to my questions were *valid* ones—the real reasons, the *right* reasons—was because I wanted to know if I was supposed to move to Costa Rica.

Paul wanted to sell our land. If I wanted to keep the Costa Rica dream alive (albeit in ICU), I needed to come up with some serious cash to buy out his half, and I needed to do it quickly. So, the question then became not just, *Did I want to live in Costa Rica someday?* or even, *Did I want a vacation oasis in Costa Rica?* But it was, *Did I want my Costa Rica dream bad enough to sell my rental house?*

I needed to know if it was my true calling to go there.

Was that me being authentic? Or was it just cool? Because if it was, that was totally fine.

But I might not sell my house for "just cool."

CHAPTER 56

write write

Julian lay on my floor. My hardwood floor. It was night. He was humming his symphony and reading *The Handmaid's Tale*. I didn't know where to go to write anymore. To process life's griefs and sorrows—the big ones that stopped my breathing and sent me to bed with my clothes on, and the little ones that I just wanted to vent about.

I took a platform class to streamline my blogs and website, to make them more "professional," but then, I didn't have anywhere else to *write write*. *Write write* my heart. But maybe. *Maybe maybe* I should just write write, anyway. Platform be damned. There was something to be said about writing as I was —showing up on the page—and whosoever gelled with the message would stay to read. Would feel the resonance. Would soak up my words, like rain, and plant their own seeds because of what I'd said. Those were the people I wanted reading my stuff anyway.

The other ones—the ones who took umbrage with my phrases, my pictures of story—those ones, they could just *not* read. They could put the book down. They could click away.

They could unfriend me. Not with any haste or malice. Just because they didn't find what I said interesting. It didn't make them bleed or cry or say, Yes. And that was okay. I wasn't writing to those people.

I'd been dancing lately. Unpeeling myself and looking inside. Sometimes the beauty in there amazed me. Other times, the dishonesty and ignorance startled me. The blindness. The self-defeating practices. (I was still lying to myself—just not as often.)

Even then, I was struggling. Struggling to write those few words, because I was blocked again. Blocked by my arrogance. My denial. My own unhealthy practices. (Who knew that not eating enough calories, or subsisting on restaurant food and instant oatmeal, and not going to bed by 10:00 p.m. could interfere with my writing?)

But there it was.

So I was forcing it through.

Sucking the stories and truths out of my bone marrow to look at them.

Thinking.

Trying not to think.

Feeling.

Trying not to feel.

And then realizing I had to.

Earlier that night, Julian and I talked about letting go of static ways of being, honoring the grieving process no matter what it was about, and then looking at ways to bring myself back to wholeness.

He said that I couldn't grow with fear stopping me every time I opened up a little, but wasn't fear a natural reaction to change? Wasn't fear a necessary emotion during transition? One that helped me slow down my impulse to sprint through the grieving process? Because that was my inclination. Hurry up and grieve. And in doing so, I missed the lessons and gratitude my life situations had gifted me. I wanted to meander, not sprint. Even if my fear was paralyzing, wasn't that better than the alternative?

Ultimately, I knew that the fear would subside with time, and I would move again. Look at the light again. Foster hope again. Actually, I believed that would happen sooner than I expected, but the safety of fear and paralysis were comforting.

If even a little annoying.

And then. And *then then*. Maybe after I had the courage to leave the sameness and routine of fear—I could *write write* again.

Platform be damned.

CHAPTER 57

experiential dance

Ecstatic dance fueled me. It was my therapy. It was my church. It was how I communicated with myself. How I listened to myself. I was so glad Julian talked me into it.

With all the angsty long-distance-boyfriend blues clinging to me, I set off to Dance one morning, intent on centering myself, tapping into a smarter part of myself. The music started, and I moved.

Most days I only danced one thing. This day, I danced uncertainty, frustration, and willingness. Danced openness, letting go, and surrendering. I danced joy, concentration, trust, grounding, and symbiosis, plus nurturing and connection with both the Divine and my peers on the dance floor.

It was exhausting and beautiful. All those emotions and sensations tumbling around and spilling out—all in one dance.

At the beginning of my Dance Church, I had felt the not-quite-frantic feeling I got when I thought about my life's purpose. I danced *"What's my calling?" "Is this my calling?"*

"What's my calling?" "I'm trying to find my calling." Calling, calling, calling. Like an echo, unanswered.

Then I sank into the music and let go. Let go of the control I so mistakenly believed I had. I surrendered to the Divine.

"*Use me as you will. Use me as your instrument in this glorious orchestra, to make beautiful music—to dance and live my joy,*" I beamed out telepathically to Whatever was listening, like a prayer.

I knew it was the only way to *find that calling*. Dance, let go, and surrender. Rinse and repeat.

The knowledge of what it felt like to be joyful and to live my purpose and answer my call sank into me. I knew what it felt like because I'd danced it already.

"*If you want me to open myself up—to show up for work and play and calling, and more important, to stop being in charge—you'll have to hold me up, be my strength, and guide me,*" I said to Whomever while dancing.

Giving myself up to the Divine Universe was scary, and it became clear through my dancing (or through the portals of dance—those shamanic dream gates) that it was a dance of giving up control, letting go of the awkwardness and fear, surrendering, accepting the Universe's promise of support, and trusting its support would be there when I leapt.

Like the flyers in Acro-yoga who needed to trust their bases. The bases could only do their job when the flyers were confident in their bases' ability to *do* their job and hold the flyers in safety.

While dancing that day, Universe gently reminded me that there would be dark places where I danced, and in those places I'd need to make sure I was paying extra close attention to staying connected to Source.

Today, everything I needed, I received.

I was still convinced, over and over, that things happened for a reason. I went in to Dance that day with expectations and a specific desire to talk to Julian, but he wasn't there. Had he been, maybe his presence would've distracted me from the meaning I was meant to receive.

CHAPTER 58

Experiencer

In a lot of ways, I felt like I was being born again. I was ready. Excited. Full of anticipation. Growth. Change. But also, the breathlessness of anxiety—like a gust of wind that took my breath away. Smacked in the face.

While I was married to Paul, I had gone to school to become a licensed massage therapist. I'd let my license lapse after a year because it was too hard to find childcare. I homeschooled only Robert at the time and he was too old for day care.

Now, I'd decided to reactivate my inactive massage therapy license. Here we go. Growth!

I challenged myself to a renewed mission of authenticity and self-honesty. And courage. Courage to say what was on my mind.

To live the way I felt inside.

To inhale life and breathe out art.

To really focus on personal growth, building creative castles in my skies, talking with people, and awakening after an autumn of disappointment--a winter of depression.

To rediscover what things caused me to *live* inside.
Seek answers within.
Welcome people to
See the Real me.
Embolden.
Emblazon.
Create art with no Rules.

~

"Do you want to be an experiencer of life? Or do you want to build something and watch it grow?" Nazim asked me once.

A leading question. I knew he wanted me to build something (slowly) with him. But right then I wanted to experience. I had spent years building something with Paul. I'd *had* that experience. Now I wanted to experience something else.

Well, why can't I have both?

Who was stopping me? It'd only be me. I *could* have both. I could experience life with a partner, and I could *build* a life with someone who wanted to grow and *experience* that life. Someone who took risks with me and created new worlds and breathed art with me.

Someone who lived and experienced the creative process *through* living.

I could have both.

In fact, I *demanded* both.

Mild alarm tingled in my extremities.

Maybe Nazim wouldn't be that for me.

But I loved him. Anger popped up and shushed me. *And how.*

"You don't just give up on people when you don't get your

own way. You make sacrifices. That's what you do. That's how it's done," some strict part of me said.

But what about the self-honesty and courage I promised myself?

How could Nazim and I exist together? Did we even really want the same things?

A quiet, sick, smoldering clung to me for the rest of the day.

CHAPTER 59

dance interlude

At Dance, which was themed Possibilities, I cried. I felt dreadful. Cold. Icy. Heavy. I sat at the back of the dance hall with my eyes closed, sort-of praying, and Jake came over.

He surprised me with a hug. He held me for about half a song, and then he went to get a drink of water from the fountain in the hall.

I tried dancing again, but I just wasn't feeling it that day. I stayed in the dance hall until the end because one reason I came to Dance was to get out of my head. To be in my body.

Writing was in my head, and the theme of Possibilities, which I assumed was for inspiring people to dream, was only calling to mind the possibility that a partnership with Nazim was not possible in the way I still wanted.

I wanted to dance into my body and feel the truth *there*, instead of listening to my Know-It-All brain, but there I was again, at the page, having pulled my journal from my purse, spewing the words from my mind.

I missed Nazim. I wanted him in my daily life, but I

couldn't have that. It didn't seem possible. It wasn't one of my options. So what did I want instead?

Time to check *in* instead of check out.

I scrawled a note in my journal, ripped it out, and danced it to the altar.

I am afraid of the possibilities.

CHAPTER 60
writer's block

Sometimes, I felt inspired to write or paint or sculpt. But sometimes, I only felt the longing to create, and couldn't experience the release of creation. Like a nightmare where you can't scream but know that if you try with all that is in you, you could make enough noise to wake up, to cast your voice out among the billions who also trudge this land. To maybe make a difference.

There was an ache when I felt unable to create my art, a loneliness that wiggled inside my brain so that it hurt, and in my throat so that I couldn't communicate.

Sometimes, while writing, my fingers would freeze at the page, clamped desperately around the pen. My breath would stop as I waited for the timid kernel of inspiration to share itself through me—but alas, Inspiration or Idea or even Plot Device did not appear, only Clamminess, Brick Wall, Pettiness, Fatigue, and Not Good Enough.

The metallic, sour taste of Lethargy and Self-Judgment sat with me when the longing to create art was strongest. I asked these soul-sucking companions why they visited; sometimes I got a response and sometimes not.

How could I rid myself of them? They were like the slugs on my sugar snap peas that ate holes before I got a taste of them.

Should I simply share space with those evil shadows of myself and honor their place in my house? What if I extended love to them, accepted them and knew there was an ancient lesson they came to teach me, if only I would listen?

Depression and Anxiety were like children with special needs. I placated them, suckled them and found their triggers to tantrums. I sat with Depression and rocked him to sleep with haunting music lilting from iTunes across the room; I coaxed Anxiety out to play—broke out the glue and treeless paper and collaged until she was more grounded.

I discovered their strengths and weaknesses and took time out for myself when they became too much for me to bear alone. I nurtured myself with popcorn and movies under the feather blanket, hot tea with a friend, or an afternoon alone at a coffee shop with my laptop and latte. And I thought. I took time to feel.

When I did that—when I gave myself permission to emote—only then was I open enough to welcome ideas and plans and as-of-yet formless characters into the sacred circle I had created for them. Only then was I able and willing to give birth to their stories.

But that wasn't right either. I was always willing. That yearning to write and to create was always there, but maybe the readiness was not.

Maybe I needed to coddle Depression and Anxiety before I could create. But ... I didn't believe I needed to be depressed or suffer anxiety attacks in order to create art. Art lived in me. I breathed it as air and it was bound to the molecules within me. I bled my art. I *was* art.

I didn't need to *be* depressed to create art, but perhaps when I was struggling with Depression at some particular time, I must *sit* with it first before I attempted to express an emotion through art that I did not yet understand. Only if I took time to nurture myself, to Think, to Feel, to *ask* Depression why he had another nightmare, to *ask* Anxiety why she cried today when the house was a mess—maybe then I could unfreeze my fingers and find my voice and let it roar with all the passion and longing and creativity I had.

And then I could create. I could write, paint, and sculpt. I could communicate and breathe and love myself again. All the parts of me. Even the shadowy ones.

CHAPTER 61

creative people feel

That winter, I looked through some old content on my blog and recognized a certain openness that didn't seem to exist there anymore. The same was true on Facebook. I wasn't posting in either place. Or, I was, but in a vanilla sanitized way. Not too emotional. Not too raw. Not too edgy. Not too... real.

Was I losing my voice?

Was I fearing judgment?

Were too many people looking?

I used to search for ways to display my character, to illustrate and show what the real me was like underneath the "stage persona." I put all of me in cyberspace for anyone to see. It was a living lesson in letting go of my fear of judgment. Now, I was censoring myself—not putting photos up on Facebook and not writing about my crazy ass emotions anymore. *Why?*

It smacked of dishonesty. *Self* dishonesty. I was lying to others by not sharing what was going on in my world. I wasn't being honest with myself, and I'd promised—no more lying to myself.

I wasn't *owning* my emotions, as if my fears and worries and joy and love didn't exist when I didn't document them. And I wanted to live with all my emotions. Even the crappy ones. I wanted to own them and examine them and feel them ... and yes, write about them. Tell the truth to myself about myself.

Maybe I could do that in a private journal, and I did, but in some big way that was also small, I felt that a person's emotions *were* their art. And the telling and showing of those emotions that could so easily get caged inside was—in fact—also art. Of course it was.

When I looked at a painting, I saw the artist's emotions, or at least their opinion about something. Even if it was a portrait, emotion was still present in the eyes and facial features of the model. The artist had painstakingly captured the subject's emotions and told the truth of their existence.

All I wanted to do was tell the truth of my emotions, express myself from the inside out. At the bottom of it, art is telling stories and truths. Even the lies of fiction have truths in them.

So why the writer's block?

Unfortunately, there was no interesting epiphany. I already knew the fucking answer. Plain old boring fear. Fear of being judged for my words/experiences/feelings. Judged by strangers. By people who said they were my friends. By my real friends. By my children. By my family. And by my lover. All of them.

"Creative people *feel*," a friend once said. "They feel deeply. And not just about the good stuff, but about the other stuff, too."

She didn't think most people understood that. Or wanted to. They just wanted to look at the pretty stuff *after* the feeling deeply part. The part that actually made the art come out.

She was right.

My certain brand of writer's block for this past year had been the fear of showing the feeling deeply before the art comes out part of creativity. And when I looked at that fear, I slammed the door shut quick. And dead-bolted it.

And really, how could art come through *that*?

Huh. I guess there was an epiphany there, after all.

CHAPTER 62

living my truth

The earth was gray and neutral, like a soggy autumn, but really it was winter. I sat in my kitchen, on the second day of the new year 2012. I'd meant to spend my New Year's Eve tallying up the lists of things I wanted to accomplish during the year. Instead, Julian unexpectedly came home early from a trip and joined me for wine and dancing in my living room. Tamara was with her kids.

When the clock read midnight, Julian and I lit candles in the dark and set our intentions for the coming year. I held his hands, said, "And so it is," and then threw open the door to let the new year come in.

We watched a couple of fireworks explode a block or two away, then settled on the couch to watch a movie. It was a delightful New Year's Eve. And I didn't write any resolutions.

However, in my white and smoky-peach colored kitchen with green slate tiles on the floor, and all my windows uncovered to let the sun show bravely through the gray sky, I wrote my intention (not resolution) for the year.

To live my truth, every moment, even if it was scary. (*No more lying.*)

To dance
To unleash
To walk in awe
Of beauty
To pray
And honor the art
That I found underneath
The layers of that opaque film that covered our daily world,
The one that most only saw up until,
I wanted to see beyond.

How I was to "live my truth" came out differently than I said it on that day in my kitchen, but that was the essence.

I thought about the unfolding I'd been doing the last two or three weeks. A metamorphosis was happening. I wasn't out of the chrysalis yet, but cells were definitely changing.

And I thought the metamorphosis was because of Dance.

It seemed slightly embarrassing and cliché to say that joining the ecstatic dance community in Eugene was transformative. But there it was. The WOW Hall on 8th and Lincoln had become my church.

Dancing every week with them had brought me more into my body—unsticking the stuck stuff. I was less in my head now. And while I was there, I thought about things in pictures. Or if the lists still came, they were lists of things that brought joy and ... bouncing. And who didn't want more bouncing in their spirit?

Writing. Poetry. Photography. Music. Words. Incense. Bangles. Fountains. Praying.

"Do you pray?" I asked Julian that New Year's Eve night.

He stopped, jolted out of what he was doing, and looked at the ceiling.

"It depends on what you mean by pray." He laughed. "Either all the time, or, no."

It was a brilliant answer.

I found myself wanting to pray—part of this transformative dance work, no doubt—and not knowing quite how to do it. Or why I wanted to do it. But, newly, I wasn't upset in the not knowing, and that felt pretty good. I was enjoying (and I must confess, slightly amused by) that foray into "praying" again. It was funny to even consider it. I had been happily "without God" for years.

Anyway.

Finding God was not my New Year's resolution. Nor intention.

Living my truth every day was my intention—a much harder task, actually. Living my truth everyday involved knowing who I was, what I stood for, and *why* I stood for it. It involved a sense of awareness. Always scanning for ways in which I wasn't living rightly—and by rightly, I meant right to myself. It involved walking in dark places on purpose because passing through the shadows would lead to personal growth. A more real me. A truer me.

And that was all I wanted for that year. To solidify the truest Me I had the strength for. To be emotionally courageous. And to remember that the truth of me changed over time. I was my own living document.

And if I was aware enough, I would actively live that change—live that truth *as* it changed.

CHAPTER 63

Necessities

Much later that year, on a summer day in the house that Humphrey loved, I had a silent, very short, mini mental breakdown. But only for an hour and a half.

I totally lost perspective—worrying about my cluttered house, my overwhelming life, Costa Rica angst, working multiple jobs, and needing more clients. Nazim called it "Paralysis by Analysis." Whatever it was, it sure made me sleepy.

I basically ran to my bed. Except, run was too energetic of a word. It was more like ... I don't know how, but I just appeared at my bed and I fell into it and completely covered my head and body with pillows and covers and slept for an hour. When I awoke, I didn't feel so panicky, but I sort of felt afraid to get up. It just sounded so exhausting.

My back door was open and flies were buzzing around, but I didn't have the energy to get out of bed to shut the door. I felt like crying. I felt achy and despondent, and I didn't want to go to work the next day. I just wanted to write and blog and move away. Maybe sleep some more.

I wanted to buy camping gear with the remaining money I had in my checking account and get plane tickets for the kids and myself and just go camping on our Costa Rica lot for the month before school started.

When I finally got up, I moved a bunch of furniture around. I was pretty sure the breakdown was over or it never really happened, and I was just tired.

I actually moved my furniture around a lot. I liked the variety. I liked the new flow of energy. I liked how the house ended up being—or at least *looking*—cleaner because of it.

On that melt-downy day, I tried to simulate living in a small space. I'd fallen prey to the Tiny House Movement and was reading all I could about it and watching cool documentaries that inspired me to live with less.

Could I prepare and eat food, rest, work, entertain, and sleep all in the same room? Yes. I found I could.

I moved my couch into the dining room and moved the dining room table into the middle of the room. After tweaking a few things, I didn't know if I liked it yet, and I wasn't actually sleeping there, but I could. And that was the point.

My next five-year plan included slowly getting rid of furniture and *things* that just cluttered up my life. Eventually, I wanted to move into consecutively smaller and smaller homes until I was only living in a tiny footprint. A smaller house equaled smaller utility bills, less housework, and fewer headaches.

However, tiny living meant less family heirloom furniture and fewer emotional attachments to inanimate objects.

Letting go of emotional attachments would probably take me a few years. But that was okay; I had five years to do it.

CHAPTER 64

tamara triggering

I had a tough day. Work at the restaurant was hard. Fast and busy. All my muscles were twanging and biting. My boss had been emotional and sad and scared. Something personal, she said. But it carried over to me and I held that sadness and fear, too—though I'm sure she didn't intend that.

And Tamara.

Oh, my heart.

"So, it turns out I've got moderate pre-cancerous cells throughout my cervix," she told me that afternoon over the phone.

She said it like she was reading from a report—so stoic and nonchalant. My diaphragm seized up, and I forced the air from my lungs to speak.

"What happens now?" I squeaked.

"I have to have a medical procedure. They say it's fairly common."

"Common?" My heart galloped and twisted in my chest, and I wanted to throw up.

"I looked it up. It's called LEAP, or something. Basically, a doctor scrapes out a lining of my cervix and takes out all those cells," she said.

I could hear her smoking a cigarette, talking around the tobacco and nicotine, giving her words a gaseous texture. I imagined them floating in the air, bumping into each other.

"When?" I could only muster up one word at a time. Sweat gathered under my arms and along my hairline. I reminded myself to breathe.

Tamara blew out smoke in an exasperated rush in my ear, like a laugh, but not. "It's expensive. I've filled out the Bridge Assistance paperwork to pay for the procedure. But there's some sort of delay."

My best friend. I closed my eyes. My single-mother-to-three-very-young-children best friend. My single-mother-to-three-very-young-children, now-in-school-on-student-loans-with-no-job best friend.

I struggled to pay all my bills and buy food for my kids on my part-time waitress wages plus tips, plus any editing work I could get on the side. And I'd even had to get a couple of free food boxes from St. Vincent de Paul's twice. I cried and raged in shame for days about that.

"I'll sell my house," I blurted.

"What?" She did laugh then. A bark. "What are you talking about?"

"I'll sell my Albany house to pay for it. Your procedure. You shouldn't have to wait. It's dangerous."

I was practically panting by then. I paced through my kitchen, tears welling and my throat closing.

"Val."

It was one word. And I stuffed my fist into my mouth to prevent even my very best friend from hearing me cry. *Who am I?* I shook my head and sniffed.

"I will," I said. "If you need the money, I'll sell. You're worth it."

And then I let her know I was crying. I could hardly prevent it. My voice did all sorts of unattractive pitches and rolls after that.

"Valerie. Oh, my god," she whispered.

Perhaps I'd surprised her, but every word was Truth. She deserved it. She deserved health care and love and comfort. I knew she had to be scared, even if she didn't show it or share it with me.

"It's okay. I'm fine. Women deal with this all the time. I don't have cervical cancer. It'll be okay."

I still paced, but I slowed. Soothed. Then, sat down at the kitchen table. I wished *I* had a cigarette, but I'd quit a decade prior when I was pregnant with Robert. The day Rob died. I sniffed again.

"Once the paperwork goes through, I'll make the appointment. It's just pre-cancerous. It's not cancer."

I'd had a pre-cancerous mole removed once. I got the news from the doctor a few days after Rob died. I had to go in for the removal a week later.

Maybe Tamara's news had triggered something in me. That old fear and grief and ... ridiculous anger that I had to deal with something like that right after Rob's death. When there was no comfort to be had. And I didn't know when it would return. If ever.

"I want to come with you," I said. "For the procedure."

A pause. Maybe a nod through the phone line. I sniffed again and scrubbed my face, wiping away the fear.

"Yes. Okay. I'd like that," she said.

CHAPTER 65
lucid dreaming

Valentine's Day approached, and as an afterthought, I drew a Faerie card from my oracle deck before going to sleep. It had been a while since I'd heard from the Fey, and I'd had a somewhat emotionally and energetically tiring day—it seemed an appropriate thing to do.

I drew The Journeyman card, in reverse, which meant I was preventing myself from doing something/going somewhere/making a change out of fear.

Very apt, since my day had entailed journaling *once again* about Nazim and how to let go of my romantic attachments and expectations *with specific outcomes*—the fantasy future I'd been pining over for more than a year.

So, I went to sleep with The Journeyman, as Mentor, traveling through my dreams.

∽

IN MY DREAM, I WAS DEAD. I WAS MARRIED WITH TWO children and a delightful house with friendly neighbors. I didn't know how I died; it wasn't important. As I died, I thought, "Okay, I'll just stay here and look over my awesome, loving family. I'll be a friendly ghost and they will always sense my comforting presence and know that I loved them."

So life carried on for them. They did their thing, and I was there. But here was the thing. Whenever I was in the room with them, the longer I stayed, the more danger they were in.

They weren't aware of the danger. There was no drama about impending doom, but I could see the room they were in begin to sink. Or, like, an invisible water was rising and covering their bodies.

I'd fly into the sky over the house, and everything would right itself. The children could move freely and weren't slowed down without knowing why. They were happier and safer without me.

I stayed and visited the house and the children many more times. Each time, much to my disbelief, I watched my family threatened by unknown peril because of me. I was making it worse for them by staying. I wanted to watch over them and bring them peace and love from the afterlife/afterworld/otherworld, but the reverse was happening. Even if they didn't know it.

On one occasion, the invisible waters were up to their chins, and I knew I had to say my goodbyes. I was frantic—feeling I hadn't had sufficient time to make sure they knew I loved them and they would be okay without me. And I was so curious to see them do their things and go about their living. I loved them. I wanted to still be a part of their lives, even though I was dead.

But as the waters unmercifully clung to them and put them in danger, I whispered a fervent *I Love You! Goodbye!* and flew straight up and out of the house.

I hovered above the roof and wondered and waffled, but I

knew if I truly loved them and wanted them to thrive, I had to let them go and trust that they still knew I loved them (and would fondly remember me). So, I flew off and away from that home, and let them live.

And I felt joy.

After the dream, I remembered—still asleep — that I *had* to remember this. I had received a message from Fey, and it directly related to my long-distance romantic relationship and the next step in my life. So I repeated, as if I was telling someone else about it, my dream. In my dream. In the inter-dream.

CHAPTER 66

allie moss

One day, not long after the lucid dream (or maybe it was before), I was in my bathroom, combing my hair or brushing my teeth. Something mundane. Nothing special. On my sound system, which was really my laptop hooked up to two crackly external speakers, a CD played. Allie Moss.

I had listened to that Allie Moss CD countless times. But that day, I heard *Prisoner of Hope* for the umpteenth time, and my ears opened.

Words from the song, lyrics I'd sung before dozens of times, spoke right to me. And I listened to them in a way I'd never done before.

I burst into tears.

Why now? I'd heard these same lines dozens and dozens and dozens of times. And I'd never cried from them before.

I needed to hear those lyrics on that day for a particular reason. I stopped what I was doing and listened to the lines again. And I cried some more.

The song said I needed to listen to myself, to the part of

myself that was older than I was. The part of myself that was ancient. The part of myself that knew what I was doing wrong in my life right then and knew how to make it better.

And the thing, the thing that I'd been driving away and avoiding in my journal and worrying about and refusing to look at, was The New Jersey Boyfriend. Nazim.

The synchronicity of the lucid dream, Allie Moss song, my growth through Dance, and the clarity to come emblazoned the truth with a capital T across my soul.

It was time to end the relationship. For real this time. (*Truth.*)

I needed to be whole and true to myself. It hurt me to be in that relationship. It hurt me to scrape together what I needed from a man who was distant from me. Maybe only geographically, yes, but still. I would not get what I wanted from Nazim, ever. And I cried that day in the bathroom because I knew it was true. I couldn't hide from it anymore. (*Truth.*)

So I dried my eyes and blew my nose and brushed my teeth. I listened to the next song on the CD and the next. I cleaned my house and did regular things.

But my world totally changed that day. I wasn't going to lie to myself about it anymore.

I could pretend a long, long time that I didn't know what was wrong or that I didn't know how to make things better. But once I looked inside and acknowledged that, yes, in fact I did know what was wrong and how to fix it, then I couldn't rewind and go back to the place where I didn't know. I couldn't go back to pretending that I didn't have that knowledge inside me.

I knew. And so I had to act.

CHAPTER 67

oh, clarity

Pine needles stuck with pitch to my sandals. I was on a field trip with Clover in Eastern Oregon at the end of May. Clover had been struggling with their own invisible disorders—misophonia (or selective sound sensitive syndrome), delayed sleep phase disorder, and social anxiety—but I believed their environment at the Waldorf school was mostly nurturing and accommodating. Robert was with me and we were staying in a cabin for a few days with Clover's Waldorf class to take part in a regional Greek Games for the fifth graders.

Unplugged, I sat in a padded lawn chair under a tree, swiping at mosquitoes, trying to let go of the last vestiges of the city's hurry and worry. I found it hard to do, possibly because my brand new iPhone sat on my lap, reminding me I had homework and client work back home.

I hadn't slept well the night before, but it was okay now in the crisp air with a wool scarf and sweater and fingerless mittens I'd knitted myself.

The staff prepared the field for the Games, the priests practiced their opening movements, and the children waited in the cold for breakfast.

My journal and book called to me, as did the birds from the neighboring trees.

Hot chocolate and breath steamed into the morning air.

Cooking staff and volunteers rang the triangle for breakfast, and I gathered my son from his play. Clover sat with their class and Robert and I enjoyed more hot chocolate with our scrambled eggs.

About eleven years and eight men ago, I dated my neighbor. He was the first man I dated after Rob died. I wanted him. He was great. He laughed at himself and the goofy antics we got up to. He sang, he wore CK cologne, he smiled, and he shaved his head. I saw a future with him. We sat in the hot tub. He slept over, fed my baby son, and put my toddler to bed. We watched football on the family room couch in our pajamas. He kissed like a dream. We drank together, did errands together, compared music, and talked talked talked.

I wanted to marry him.

But he wanted to be just friends. Which was confusing to me because whenever he'd come over to "watch a movie," we'd end up having sex. And every time we ended up having sex, I thought, "Maybe now he'll want to be my boyfriend."

He always felt bad after we made love. Not right then, of course, but the day after. He'd call me or email me and explain again that it just wasn't fair to me to keep having sex because he didn't see a future with me. He just wanted to be my friend.

I'd say, "Yeah, yeah, sure, okay." And the next time we'd get together, I'd ply my femininity and use my hands, and he would breathe faster, and we would join again.

"I wish you liked me more," I said one day.

He pulled me to himself and pulled off my clothes.

"I like you too much. If I didn't like you as much as I do, I would have sex with you, no problem."

Somehow, this didn't seem contradictory to us making love right then.

"Let's just try it. Please. I know I could make you a good girlfriend. You know you already like me, you know you already like what I do to you ..."

So he finally caved.

For two weeks.

Then he said no. No more. I just want to be friends. Period. So, we stopped having sex. He didn't visit much anymore. We started dating other people.

One day my boyfriend at the time broke up with me—*by sending me a letter in the mail*. It felt like such a loser way to break up with someone that it spilled over to me. Then *I* felt like a loser. I didn't love him, but I was still despondent over being dumped, and I wasn't even worth a *verbal* dumping. He'd sent the US Postal Service to do his dumping.

I called my neighbor over. We were still friends. He cuddled me. He made me laugh. He took my mind off the other guy. And we ended up right where you'd think we would. It was glorious. Inevitably, the thought came back.

"Maybe now he'll want to be my boyfriend."

I smiled all next morning. I smiled all next afternoon. I smiled all evening. Then, I went out to my car and drove out of my driveway. On the way out of my cul-de-sac, I saw him driving back in. We stopped and rolled down our windows to talk.

I don't remember what we said now, but whatever it was—ordinary enough, I'm sure—I had a true to god Epiphany. So true, in fact, that it didn't hurt. I even smiled when it hit me, strictly *because* of its Truth.

He didn't want to be my boyfriend.

It was a pity fuck.

He assured me years later that it was *not*, in fact, a pity fuck. He'd *wanted* to do it. For him, too. Not just me. It wasn't because he felt sorry for me. Regardless of the reason he fucked me, the reality was still the same.

He didn't want to be my boyfriend.

And I finally believed him. That was the kicker.

Somehow, I'd tricked my mind into thinking if I just could convince him with the right words, the right moves, he'd see me. But no. The realization was sweet and simple, and there wasn't any heartache afterward. It was just simply the truth. He didn't want to be my boyfriend.

I found myself in a strangely parallel storyline with Nazim. Though the backstory was much different.

The only reason Nazim was in this country legally was because he was working for a company that was *getting* him a green card. Once he'd gone far enough into the process, he could move to Oregon and we could be together.

"We could get married, though! We know we love each other. We've even briefly lived with each other. We know we're great in bed. *I* could get you the green card. Quit your job and move. We can be together *now*," I had said many, many times.

His answer was never yes.

His answer was never no.

It was always a mix of ego and fear, and wait-just-a-minute-that's-not-how-it's-done.

I kept thinking—if I just say it the right way, with the right words, with the right moves, he will see me. See what I am offering. See the life we can have. The life he *wants*.

I knew he wanted it. He said he wanted stability. He said he wanted roots, and to come home from work to the woman he loved.

He imagined our future together—even though he said it

brought him pain and anxiety to do so. He saw us on the top floor of his parents' house. He saw himself teaching me cricket. He saw having a baby with me. He saw telling his parents about me. He saw us living together.

But I guess I wasn't saying it hard enough. We'd stayed alone, on opposite sides of the country from each other, and repeated like a mantra for the broken-hearted, "The universe just has other plans for us right now." We'd been waiting for this unending green card process to continue continue continue.

But after eighteen months, we were both breaking.

Two messages looped around each other in my brain like the rounds Clover and their friends sang at school functions.

The first was the marriage message. If he would just consent to marriage, we'd be together.

The second message looping in my brain was, if you love someone ... really, truly love someone ... then you would make it work, no matter what.

Why was he really saying no to getting married? Yes, it wasn't the way he/we envisioned it happening. It wasn't as organic as we thought it would be. It had some legal red tape wrapped around a couple of the edges. But it would still get us in the same state. In the same city. With the same future ahead of us. Marriage and Family and Foreverness.

If he was repeatedly saying no (or more accurately, not yet), he must not love me as much as I loved him. It must mean, on some level, he wasn't ready for marriage. Or maybe he wasn't ready for marriage with me.

What was really going on here? I deserved to know.

Out of town at the Greek Games, without internet access, I texted Nazim.

> The only reason I'm not right there beside you is because I think it's not the best place for my kids. It would hurt people if I went there. But I often wonder who it would hurt if you came here? Why aren't you here for me?

Because of a cluster fuck.

> When you explain it to me on Skype, or in person, I mostly understand. But here, all by myself, I don't. Doubts creep in and I get confused and feel like there just must not be enough love if you are in New Jersey. Why do I feel that? Do I not understand because I don't want to?

It is because you love me and you want me very much.

> Those things are true, but what does that have to do with me not comprehending how you could stay away from me, by choice? I need my man. I don't just want and love you. I need you. You are my blood and oxygen.

I understand. I am struggling with this situation.

> I have fantasies about you showing up on my doorstep or outside my work, saying, 'I'm here now. Forever. You said to come, so I did.' And then actually staying.

I am sorry. We both have to accept our current situation. You know my visa situation.

> This is the part where the heartbreak and not understanding come in. I know you need a green card to stay in this country and I know I could get you that green card, but for some reason, you don't want it. I don't mean to sound naggy or bitchy; it's the tape that's playing over and over in my head though.

> What tape, baby?

>> The recording in my head that repeats and repeats that you don't want me enough to marry me and get the green card that will allow us to be together.

This was where I expected him to jump in and contradict me. Something akin to, "No no. I do love you! It's just that ..." Instead, I got—

>> Do you have the heart to accept our current situation and live with it?

I gasped in the thin Eastern Oregon spring air. He could've slapped my face and I wouldn't have felt any different. Maybe it was the impersonal method of texting. On Skype, I could see his eyes while he said it. Maybe he said it with compassion and angst. So I tried again. Telling it like it was from my heart.

>> What else is there to do? Except convince you otherwise. Sometimes I feel like I'm just not making my wishes and love known well enough to you. Like if I try harder you'll suddenly say 'Oh, how foolish I've been.' And then you'll come to me in my dreams and in my reality.

Again, I needed some reassurance that he really loved me and that this separation was terrible for him and he dreamt of marrying me and that the only reason he wasn't doing it was ... etc. Instead—

>> What is preventing you from accepting our situation and being happy with it?

Smack. Maybe that was still the text medium not allowing his lovely voice to caress me with his honest curiosity and concern for me, but that sentence just hurt. I stabbed the touch screen.

> Because it's not what I want. It's what I'm begrudgingly settling for. I want you to be a part of my life every day. Not four times a year.

My battery died at that point, and I was frantic to know his response. I couldn't get to my car to charge up my phone and read his answer. I took a few deep breaths and let go of knowing for a while. And what came to me was this: *my neighbor*.

My boyfriend didn't want to be married to me.

That was it. It was simple and clean. The Truth.

I'd been begging him to marry me for almost a year. I'd asked him, like, eight times. I'd figured out legal angles and pleaded with him. I'd started losing my newly gained self-respect.

And just like that day in our cars, when I smiled with the Truth about my neighbor, *He doesn't want to be my boyfriend*, I sat in the country meadow watching my gender-neutral teen in a relay race and smiled with the Truth.

He doesn't want to marry me.

No heartbreak. Just the truth. He was my lover. We had love for each other. We had luscious memories. We had mad travel adventures planned for the future, if it ever came.

But we weren't getting married.

And I'd stop asking.

And he'd stop hedging.

The smell of lasagna wafted over May breezes to haunt the pre-dinner hungry, and I refocused on Clover's Greek wresting practice, joining in with the other parental spectators.

CHAPTER 68

breaking up

A few days later, I turned Skype on, knowing what it would mean.

When Nazim came online, and I answered the Skype call, he smiled at me with his beautiful, dreamy, black Indian eyes.

We said hello and exchanged a few pleasantries while I felt awkward with what needed to come out next. I didn't want to carry on a long conversation and then spit it out. It had to come first.

"I feel done," I said.

I paused, not sure if I needed to continue or if he would know what I meant.

Sometimes it was hard to read the eyes through a long-distance computer call, but I thought I saw he understood. Even so, he questioned.

"What do you mean? Done with us?"

"Yes."

It was time for me to be concrete and unyielding, even though the things I liked about myself were my flexibility and compassion and ability to try new things and to leap into the open without fear. Despite that, fear had become such a huge part of my life that I was sick of it. I was done being afraid, and I was done not being happy, and I was done doing it all to myself.

It would've been easy to blame Nazim for my pain and exhaustion and unhappiness. It would've been easy to say that he was primarily at fault for our long-distance blues. That he could have stopped it at any time. But, so could have I. (*Truth.*)

"I'm just not having any fun anymore," I said.

My shoulders drooped down, and my heart beat slow and steady. I knew what I was saying, and I knew I wouldn't let him talk me out of it anymore. I think he knew that, too, because he only nodded with his lips closed together.

He took a deep breath and pushed it out through those full lips and scrubbed his head with his hands.

"Okay then," he said.

The next day, I cried with him again and he wanted to be clear that in no way was he mad or bitter and even that he was sharing the responsibility with me. He felt he put us in this long-distance situation in the first place. "Totally indirectly and not to blame, of course." (*Eye roll.*)

He believed that we both had come to this conclusion. That he didn't really see it as a breakup, but more as a transition.

Transition sounded infinitely better than breaking up.

We'd both been living without crucial human needs. For months and months. And it had taken its toll on us. On our minds, on our hearts, on our bodies. It had hurt us.

We'd loved each other for almost two years despite staggering challenges—my marriage, my quest for sexual identity, his job loss, his move to New Jersey, the whole dating other men thing, and all the months apart. Not to mention the "little" things. I wasn't Indian or Muslim, and he was more conservative than me. I was divorced twice, *widowed for God's sake*, had two half-grown children, and was ambivalent about having more.

Despite all that, there was love and worship and obsession and sex and play and laughter and culture and language and trust. There was tenderness and protectiveness. There was nurturing and comfort.

I loved the exotic. I loved the differences between us. I loved his accent and the way he laughed and pushed his glasses up on his nose. The way he wiggled his foot for no reason, and wore the same outfit every day when he wasn't at work or going out. Blue sweatshirt, blue hat, white t-shirt, pajama pants, black slippers.

I loved his hands and his words and the sound of his voice. It always calmed me and grounded me, even when we were disagreeing.

But we weren't alive. We lived a shadow life. One where we only came alive when we sexted each other, saw each other on Skype, talked on the phone, planned our next visit, or watched our homemade porn videos.

And the worst part? Sometimes, even those very things that made me feel alive *didn't*. They made me feel worse. Because it didn't happen in body, only in the cyberworld.

It seemed I'd hit my limitation. I didn't know I had any of those. I'd never been good at boundaries.

CHAPTER 69

write now

I felt sick that I wasn't with Nazim. I was once again staring out the window and at the tablecloth. My feet were stuck to the floor, not wanting to go to work or grocery shopping or talking to anyone. Just sitting. Just waiting. For the rocks of depression to settle on my limbs again.

"That can't happen again," I told myself firmly.

I talked to Tamara one evening in June about Nazim and closing that door, and how sad I felt. Again, I felt like I was on the right track, but it was still painful and I didn't quite know what to do with myself, how to ground this leftover energy I'd previously spent on obsessing about a future with Nazim.

The answer was to write. The answer was to heal. The answer was to grow.

But why did I feel like I was leaving him behind? Why did I feel so disloyal? Could I not stay in any relationship? Would I always be flighty? Had I used up my loyalty? Was it finite, like food?

When we talked, he said all the right things, like he was proud of us for trying so hard, and the distance was the only problem we had had. That we had splendid memories and would still be companions and friends.

Always before, when a tough decision needed to be made, I'd agonized over it. But once I'd made it, I relaxed into it. Felt relief that I had made it and made plans to carry out the new regime. But this time around, the decision made, I was at a standstill.

The answer, loud and clear, was to write. In any way it came out. Write in any fashion.

This would be my new mantra. When I heard myself asking, What do I do now?

Write.

How do I stop jonesing for the future or the past with Nazim?

Write.

Should I take down his picture?

Write.

That was all I needed to know right then.

Write.

it still hurts

In a small shelter,
Not of earth
But of my own,
Huddled in the corner
Of my psyche,
I shiver
And shake
And believe.

Survival means
Holding my breath
Until sleep comes, or
Until you reach for me and I hold out
A trembling finger
For you to touch.

CHAPTER 70

a new direction

One night, I dreamt multiple times that Rob and I talked. The first time I went to him and told him I'd been wrong. I missed him too much, and I thought we should get back together. I started babbling on to him about how it would be different and how we'd live, and Rob stopped me and said, "But I'm dead."

In another part of the dream, we might've made love. For sure, he held me.

Awake afterward, I felt worn out emotionally. I was always starting over. I had hit the wall almost at the end of the race, and if I didn't finish, none of it would be for anything.

"Make it better, or let it go," a friend told me once.

I couldn't make my situation with Nazim any better. He lived in New Jersey and couldn't or wouldn't leave, and I lived in Oregon and couldn't or wouldn't leave. So I couldn't make it better. My only other option was to let it go.

And I did. I had to.

Emotions and fears and people's talk swayed me, and I lost touch with my voice, my heartbeat. And when that happened, I lost my connection with Source, because *I* was my connection to Source.

I always thought Nature and meditation were my connection to Source, and lots of times I could access through writing, but those places and strategies were only ways of getting quiet so I could hear *me*.

Julian did a shamanic heart walk for me one evening. He saw a bird flying overhead and called it down. It was maybe a hawk or an eagle. It wouldn't talk, and Bird was not its true shape. It had lost its voice.

Julian's message was to wait. To be quiet and let the heartsickness pass on its own. That the bird was me.

CHAPTER 71

moving on

Coffee rested in one of Nazim's old mugs on the windowsill next to me. The coffee machine clicked into a restful period, and my dog alternately crunched his breakfast or licked his doggie lips and swallowed.

I'd done my *puja* and smudged the house with Nag Champa. I'd offered my prayers without words to the gods-- Ganesh, Lakshmi, the Goddess, and Durga.

Humphrey drank water, came to nuzzle me, and then waited at the back door to be let out. I didn't rise from my journal writing in the otherwise quietness of the house until I heard the bell ring. Humphrey's bell. The one he pushed with his nose, sending it swinging from the twine tied to the doorknob.

I sipped from my coffee cup and contemplated my unworded prayers in my manuscript. My cell phone signaled a text received. Delaying my prayers a little longer, I got my phone from the charger in the kitchen.

The sky was gray today, with a misting of rain, the first of the season. I was glad. My grass was dead from the heat of the summer and early autumn, and I longed for its return to the green. I wanted to redo the yard and make it a growing place again. Remove the blackberries, weed the raspberries, and tie up and stake the canes. I wanted to fix the lawn mower, get a last good mowing before the winter, and prepare two small garden beds.

My thoughts drifted back to my manuscript. *What can I put into my memoir to infuse it with The Something that will touch the reader?*

The bananas in the red ceramic bowl were spotting brown and my stream of consciousness shifted to worry about my firewood not getting split in time for the cold. It was time to prepare for winter. It was time to nest.

My unwhispered prayers that morning were: help stay connected to Source, help to check in with myself every day, and help in the continuation of the teeny, tiny forward momentum away from my fantasies.

I thought about the reason Nazim and I came together. I'd speculated on many things, but one semi–new one came up for me. *To always speak the heart's truth.* Even if it was raw, confusing, contradictory, painful, scary. Because if I did, the real hopes—the ones I didn't dare to dream—came true. Or at least had the possibility of coming true.

During our last visit together, Nazim and I had talked about sacrifice versus compromise and what we'd sacrificed for our relationship. I learned I could sacrifice for love. But when it no longer worked, when I wanted to call in my sacrifice, *it was the doing so without guilt that was the problem for me.*

Nazim told me he and his date kissed last Friday. I didn't feel jealous. It was actually nice to have the type of relationship with Nazim that would allow such a discussion. We'd reached another milestone.

I went to check my phone one more time and refilled my coffee cup before settling in to manuscript edits.

The theme at Dance the next night—conveniently enough—was letting go, but the music didn't seem to match. It was far too head-bang-y for me. Not what I felt called to dance to at all.

Afterward, Julian invited himself over for dinner, which was no problem, but he also wanted to have a potluck gathering. I felt like holing up, despite my loneliness, so I said, "Yes."

It was the only way to pull out of my depression.

Sometimes, most times, there's a point where a break happens, a place you can't bear to go anymore, a line you can't cross anymore. You are fed up with yourself, with the way things are.

Even if the approach to that line is gradual and you can't see the threshold you are crossing, you just look around suddenly and realize where you are. That you can't go back to that old way, old belief, old house, old love, old lie.

For me, it was a series of lies. Lies that I lived. And believed. But when I crossed that threshold—breaking up with Nazim—I went back. I went back to the dark place of lies. I thought, perhaps, that's where I was supposed to be.

But when I looked back at the crossed threshold and peered out into the fresh new leafy green place with no lies, the darkness behind me became dank and fetid, unbearable.

So, I stepped into the freshness, convinced this was the better place, the better way.

Despite that, I went back to the dark. But this time, I just went for my luggage.

This time, I was making a permanent move.

CHAPTER 72

manifestation

What did I really want from a romantic partner? A list came to mind. *Of course.* I always fell back on lists.

~

<u>I Want</u>

- *Passion.* I really want him to rock my world. I, of course, would reciprocate.
- *A companion for myself.* I don't need a father for my children. They already have that. More like someone that I hang out with so that I'm not lonely. A long-term relationship.
- *Someone who will be friends with my kids,* feel comfortable around them, and understand their special needs and quirks.
- *An activity partner.*
- *Artistic or creative in some way.*

- *Encourages my artistic/creative side.*
- *Someone who'll baby me when I'm sick or sad.*
- *Someone who inspires me to action,* whether that's to revise my manuscript, mow a lawn, or hike Mount Pisgah.
- *Someone to get me and my kids outdoors more often.*
- *Must like dogs,* especially punk ass ones afraid of everything. (Humphrey.)
- *Can deal with a blended family* without jealousy or fear, or if those emotions exist, then be willing and cognizant enough to talk them through.
- *Practices nonviolent, nonjudgmental communication.*
- *Loves reading.*
- *Has some spirituality* (any form) but is moderate and nonjudgmental of my lack of it (or rather, my particular eclectic brand of paganism).
- *Will tolerate my India obsession,* but preferably thinks it's secretly cute (or hell, even join me in it).
- *Builds trust evenly and steadily.* I want to look into his eyes and be drawn to staying there. I want to feel safe saying anything I need/want to say. Totally authentically, and have that reciprocated.
- *I want to play.* And dance. And camp at the Oregon Country Fair and take the kids to Faerieworlds and dress up.
- *A good kisser.*
- *Someone who doesn't mind a little mess around the house.* I'm not a great housekeeper or cook, but I like a clean house and good food.
- *If he eats Velveeta cheese or McDonald's, he's out.*
- *Will watch foreign films,* quirky, independent romantic comedies, and Jane Austen with me.

- *Will grow and evolve* into the person he is supposed to be (the one he already is inside) with or without me. And expects me to do the same.
- *Will travel with me* when my savings allow me a vacation.
- *Is okay with me having male friends.*
- *Can take better care of houseplants than me.*
- *Is okay with public displays of affection.*
- *Touches me. Always. I need touch and attention.*
- *Whatever work he does, I need weekend time with him.* No crazy workaholics, crazy work schedules, or video gamers. I'm not needy or clingy, but I need him to be available to me. Physically and mentally.
- *I can't talk politics with him,* or sports, but I love stimulating conversation about cultures, social dynamics, art, travel. My friends can talk engineering, politics, and psychology with him, though.

Bonuses

- *Speaks another language(s).* Somehow, that is super sexy to me.
- *Full lips.*
- *A big you-know-what that is used well.*
- *Buys me stuff.* I'm not materialistic, but sometimes I feel girly and want the pampering.

Final Thoughts

- Self-deprecation is charming, but low self-esteem isn't.

I RE-READ THE LISTS. TWICE.
And then several more times.
Then, I put them away.
And so it is.

CHAPTER 73

first date with ali

I met Ali through OkayCupid.com.
The first time I met him in person was at Davis's Restaurant in Eugene, Oregon. It was on the tenth month, on the ninth day, at 8:00 p.m. It was how we remembered our anniversary day for many years.

10, 9, 8.

I met him on a Tuesday night after Dance. I wore a black long-sleeved t-shirt and a pair of jeans. My hair was long and brown at the time and I had a *dupatta* wrapped around my neck. He was sitting at the table, waiting for me, reading *The Color Purple* by Alice Walker. His hair was long, too, to his shoulders. Both of those realities—the long hair and the reading of Alice Walker—made me smile even before he raised his eyes to mine.

He smiled back when he saw me, used a bookmark to hold his place (I always folded pages) and laid the book on the table. He stood as I approached. He already impressed me.

During our evening together, we told each other our stories, and Ali shared his mother's story as well. It was heartbreaking.

She was a woman who was strong and resilient despite sorrow and really shitty things happening to her.

I teared up during the telling of it and he told me later that it was a determining moment for him. He wanted to know this woman who would cry with compassion for his mother, a woman she'd never met. And maybe never would.

I played with my hair. I played with my scarf. Trying to seduce him without looking like I was seducing him. (I think he guessed I was.)

We shared pictures of our dogs from our cell phones. At one point I got up from my chair and came around to his side and laid on the bench next to him, with my head in his lap. I was a little buzzed, but he didn't seem to mind.

He was creative. He was a printmaker, a musician, and also a writer. A technical one. He would never make fun of me for loving to write and feeling called to it. He would never deny me time to work on my art.

He enjoyed dancing, and boy, howdy, so did I.

His mom lived in India for part of every year! *How's that for a bonus?* I could now thoroughly enjoy my Indophile tendencies without guilt or embarrassment.

He liked travel, outdoor activities, and *dogs*. I would never again have to apologize for the dogs in my life.

"It's actually a deal-breaker for me," he said. "Any woman I'm with has to love dogs."

"No problem there," I assured him.

I didn't know it yet, but my life was about to be so much fuller. The depression I struggled with was about to be way more manageable with Ali in my life. We cared for each other when one of us was low, and we encouraged each other when one of us faltered.

At the end of the night, Ali walked me to my car, and we hugged.

CHAPTER 74

second date with ali

For our second date, I invited Ali over to Bollywood Night—the first time he'd be at my home. Bollywood Night took place roughly every month. It was an open invitation, potluck-style, and I played a Bollywood movie. Bollywood music played during the intermission, and I gave out bindis to wear if I had them. Sometimes I wore *salwar kameez* dresses from work.

"You're sure you won't be too bored? Bollywood movies are long."

"No." He smiled and touched my arm. "I used to watch them with my mom. She likes them. I do, too. They're so innocent."

When Ali arrived, he brought out presents. *Who was this man?*

He brought me a bottle of wine, and—major points given—he brought Humphrey (whom he'd not met yet) a bag of dog treats. Organic ones. *Awww.*

I sat on the floor at Ali's feet and circled my arm around his leg during the movie just to have contact. I wanted to look into his eyes and for him to seduce me. I would not have sex with him on Date Two. That's not what this was all for. But I wanted to get to the part of the night where everyone would leave, so I could have Ali all to myself.

But after the movie, after most had left, one lady remained. Maybe oblivious. Maybe lonely. Who knows? Maybe this was her only night out without her kids in a long time. No judgment, but I was desperate for her to leave.

She sat at the kitchen table and smiled and laughed and talked and shared her delicious food. I remember there was Adjvar and feta cheese on bread. So, so yummy. And olives. There were always olives at my house. One thing Ali said he liked about me was my love for olives.

We still laugh about that together.

When my friendly acquaintance left, Ali brought out a couple of books he wanted to share. One of them was a book of Turkish poetry by Ataol Behramoglu. We sat on the couch—me with my head in Ali's lap—and he wooed me with that Turkish poetry.

"Yaşadiklarimdan ögrendigim bir şey var ..."

He said his father had wooed his mother with Turkish poetry, too.

After poetry, we made out. I took off my shirt. We didn't have text book sex, but we did everything else. Which was still sex, now that I think of it. Orgasms were had. It was a delicious night.

We sat, intertwined and sweaty, on the couch, half undressed.

"You're so beautiful," he whispered, "that you practically ooze sex."

I sat up straighter, both delighted and somehow embarrassed.

"And I'm not saying that just because you gave me a blowjob."

We laughed a long time after that, and after we'd dressed, he wooed me again with his Turkish poetry.

We made plans to introduce the dogs. He would come to my home in the morning before work and the dogs would meet during a walk.

I was giddy with newness. With possibility. It felt good to wear possibility instead of the heavy chain mail of depression. (*Truth.*)

CHAPTER 75

dreamy

I felt ...dreamy. I thought about Ali all the time. Couldn't wait to see him. I texted him multiple times each day. Imagined future scenarios and brainstormed more ways to spend time with him.

I wondered what his regular schedule looked like before I started taking up all his time.

It all felt suspiciously like love, but it was too soon for that.

CHAPTER 76
"*you match.*"

While Ali and I had had sleepovers before, it was the first one that coincided with when the kids were over, and I was a little worried about what they would think. Robert, especially, had disliked Nazim.

I wouldn't give the kids veto power, but I couldn't imagine having to maneuver around child hostility with the man I was with. It was important to me for them to like Ali.

Tamara came over the next morning, too, on purpose. I wanted the house full and for it to somehow magically seem normal that Ali was there.

It seemed strange that it hadn't already happened, but somehow it was the first time that Ali and Tamara would meet, too. I wasn't worried that she wouldn't like him, though. How could she not?

I was more anxious for the meeting to take place, so that we could slip into Three Musketeer status. All for One and One for All, and all that. I wanted Tamara to be family for Ali, like she was for me. We were Soul Sisters, because we both had a blood sister who didn't care for us. We'd adopted one another.

When Tamara arrived, and I made the introductions, she smiled and hugged and did all the normal things one does when meeting important people. We interacted for a few minutes more while Ali played with Tamara's ukulele, let Humphrey in and out, talked with the kids, served coffee, and lounged on the couch. And then Tamara sat up and smiled really big.

"You match," she said.

She actually *cooed* it. *You match.*

Which was the perfect thing to say. She saw it. She saw why I fell for him so quickly. Ali and I *did* match.

My face warmed, and my fingertips tingled.

In fact, in my memory, this was the first thing out of her mouth, but my brain says it couldn't have been. Later, I *assumed* she had said all those necessary how-do-you-dos first.

We matched.

CHAPTER 77

not perfect: perfect

"There are so many things I like about you, Ali. You are so perfect."

We were at his place, sitting on the couch, smoking pot. He squirmed under my gaze. I traced my fingertip along his ear, and he sighed.

"You're exotic," I whispered. "You have a sexy accent."

I squeezed his arm.

"Speak to me in Turkish," I said.

"*Kendimi gözlerinde kaybettim,*" he murmured, eyes closed.

I snuggled into him.

"Why do you think I'm perfect? I'm not perfect," he said a moment later.

"Because you read me poetry, you have dogs, and you love mine. Because you're romantic. Because you like camping and love art. I love that you are an artist, too. And that you play the mandolin," I said, warming to my topic.

He frowned.

"That doesn't make me perfect."

"I know. But you communicate well, and you're an attentive lover—which I really like," I said.

He said nothing.

I sat up, wondering what was wrong. What was he thinking?

I had a load of other things I already loved about him but didn't say. Wouldn't say. Like how he was already planning things with me (plans for next summer) and dreamed of living in an intentional community (Costa Rica for the win!) and tolerated my Indian obsession—probably because his mom lived in India half the year—and I could already imagine a life with him.

"I'm afraid that the longer you know me, the less perfect I'll be," he said.

"Have you been dishonest with me? Are you misrepresenting yourself to me?" I said.

He shook his head. "No."

"Then..." I shrugged.

I leaned against him, and he held my hand.

"I'm not saying you are perfect. I'm saying that you're perfect for *me*."

He seemed much more comfortable with that.

CHAPTER 78
day of the dead

Ali stayed over on Friday nights, and he and I were snuggling in my bed on a Saturday morning. It was cold and gray. Samhain was approaching.

Ali sighed. My head, resting on his chest, moved with his breath.

"I feel closer to you knowing that you've suffered loss," he said.

I lifted my head. He knew about Rob, but I still must've looked at him strange because he grasped at my hand and held tight.

"Because I've lost people I love, too. Right?" he said. "I told you. My brother." He shook his head and looked at our hands. "He was only 21."

"Knowing about Rob tells me you understand pain," he said, his eyes soft. "That you know a little of what I've gone through in losing my brother and my dad."

I rolled over on my back.

"I usually make a Day of the Dead altar every year," I said to the ceiling. "It's to honor the people I loved who've died." I glanced at him to gauge his reaction.

I used to feel, after Rob died, that any relationship I entered was an act of betrayal. Doing the altar was a way to give Rob a defined place in my life and still be able to live in the present without the shackles of guilt and remorse. He was there, but not there.

"You want to do the altar with me?" I asked. I held my breath. *It doesn't matter if he does. I prefer doing it solo.* (*Lie.*)

Fuck! The lie slipped in. I *wouldn't* prefer doing it solo, but I was used to it. (*Truth.*)

He gathered me into a hug. My answer then. I breathed again, surprised at my relief. I hadn't shared this ritual with anyone since that time Paul refused. Often, whenever Rob came up in conversation with Paul, he'd feel so "Second" that I kept Rob inside my sleeve rather than on it. I had a feeling it wouldn't be like that with Ali.

"I wish you could've known them," he said into my hair.

I squeezed him. I didn't tell him that sometimes I imagined Aytek and Hasan standing on either side of Ali as he went about his day. Would it bring him comfort or creep him out? Or worse, would he scoff at me? Think of me with disdain? I couldn't bear that.

Before dropping off the kids at Paul's that Saturday afternoon, I gathered a few of Rob's things and pictures of my grandparents, a watch of my grandmother's, along with a pretty cloth and a candle.

I always slept over at Ali's while the kids were gone now. I had a toothbrush there and a few articles of clothing. Ali had given me a robe to keep there, too, the first time I spent the night there. Humphrey peed on his couch during our first visit, too. So we'd both left something at Ali's.

That day, with music playing on his stereo, I started assembling the altar. We decided it would go on the kitchen bar, next to a glass sculpture of a large shrimp. I laid out the cloth, and he went in search of a picture of his father. I pulled out Rob's watch, a note he had left me just before he died, and his driver's license. A sudden sob rose in my throat, and I clamped my hand over my mouth, startled.

Rob had been dead for thirteen years. Still, sometimes, my grief swatted at me, like the mean cat we had growing up who'd wait on the bookcase for someone to walk by so she could brandish her claws at the unsuspecting person. The grief would catch me by surprise, a big walloping dose of it. It would sting, and I'd rub at the grief and grouse that it still affected me after all these years.

Ali brought out his brother's hand drum, a snapshot of his dad who had died the year before, and several "card decks" of Turkish recipes. Aytek, Ali's father, had liked to cook. He arranged them all on the altar, next to Rob's dog tags and his cigarette rolling papers.

We lit a candle and sat on the couch, holding hands. We were both quiet, and then Ali wept.

"I'm a bad son," he said. He squeezed his eyes shut and his shoulders shook.

I pushed myself into his side so he could feel my warmth. I hoped it gave him silent reassurance.

"We'd been fighting. Every time I called him, we'd end up arguing." He sniffed.

"He called me right before he died. Maybe a day or two." Ali's voice stilled.

I reached for his hand. He squeezed back.

"I didn't answer the phone. I didn't want to talk to him and fight again." His voice cracked. "And then he died." He sobbed and bent forward.

I pulled him to me and held him fast. He hadn't been back

to Turkey in years and hadn't been able to make it right, make amends, before his father's aneurysm.

I really wanted to say something. I wanted to jump in and say, *No. Of course not. You're not bad.* But this was Ali's grief. I wanted to take away his pain, to ease his mental suffering, but I didn't want to take away his means of processing. I wanted to *witness* it. I didn't want him to feel judged that he was crying in front of me. I wanted to *normalize* it.

With other relationships, I made it my mission to make my men feel better. It was my job. My compulsion. Somehow, looking back, it felt tied up in the religion thing. Maybe because if I made others feel better, they wouldn't look too closely at me—find things to judge. If I was good and made others feel good, took care of others, then maybe I wouldn't get in trouble. (The elders wouldn't come a callin'.)

With Ali, instead of jumping in and "saving" him, I lay my head on his shoulder and grasped his hand again. He needed to feel it. And I would honor that. We sat without words a while longer, snuffling and wiping our faces.

"It was good," Ali said afterward. "I'm glad we did it."

I nodded. For as long as I had done the altar, it felt right to do. I was glad it was a ritual I could keep doing. That Ali would join me in doing it. That I didn't have to feel weird about it or surreptitiously continue the practice of it.

Another way Ali and I fit.

CHAPTER 79

falling in love

I fell totally head over heels in love with Ali on the day we had sex for the first time.

"Want to see some pictures?" he asked me. He had his laptop with him and his dogs, too.

We sat on the love seat in the kitchen and pushed the table out of the way. I scooted up next to him and watched as he scrolled through the photos account on his MacBook.

Show and Tell is actually a lovely way to get to know someone. He showed me pictures of his best friends, camping trips, nature photos. We stumbled upon some pictures of his most recent ex, which seemed to make him a little sad. He lamented they weren't on better terms and wished they could still be friends, but she didn't want that (or couldn't manage it).

"It's too bad," he said. "I learned a lot from her, and she really helped me out when my dad died." He blinked and sighed and forwarded through a few more photos.

After Show and Tell, we kissed and peeled off a few layers of clothes. My couch, it seemed, was an aphrodisiac.

I straddled him, skin to skin, and kissed him. His lips were warm and full and his hands tickled my ears and tugged at my lobes. I kissed more, trying to seduce him with whatever I had in my repertoire. I wanted to impress him. I'd never thought of myself as being "good in bed," though I'd had some practice.

We were both aroused and excited. It would happen tonight. We were going to have Sex for the First Time.

His hands drifted to my arms and my hips, and I ticked his jaw with my fingertips. Happy sighs and more clothing removal took place, but too soon his kisses slowed and didn't seem to have an equal amount of fervor as before.

Maybe I tensed. Maybe I sensed. Maybe there was another clue I subconsciously tuned in to.

Ali was decidedly not "there" anymore.

I pulled back and looked into sad hazel eyes.

"What happened?" I crooned. "Where did you go?"

"What do you mean?" he evaded.

"Just now. You left. We were kissing, but then something happened and you just weren't there anymore."

I felt instinctively like speaking quietly. I didn't want to spook him. His body became taut, like a prey animal ready for flight.

Ali looked uncomfortable—eyes down, arms against his belly, pulled in tight against him. Holding himself separate, even by a few inches.

I slid off his lap and sat next to him.

"I don't know," he said, softly. He offered a small smile. "I guess looking at those pictures was a bad idea."

He meant the pictures of his ex.

I took his hand.

"Then let's go snuggle," I said, gesturing to my room. I stood up. He stood up.

I indicated he go in front of me. His naked body slid around me and crossed through my bedroom doorway, hands held in soft fists by his side, hair swinging at the bottom of a pale neck.

We climbed into my bed and pulled the covers up. I snuggled into his armpit, his arm around my shoulder, mine on his chest.

And we talked. I don't even remember the topics. But we nuzzled and laughed and kissed more and talked more. And then it happened.

There was a condom and jokes about teenage dream girls and connection. Deep and satisfying, like coming home after an extensive tour.

Ali and I fit. In every way.

"October 23, 2012," Ali said.

"What?"

"It's today's date. The first time we had sex."

He said it like he wanted to enshrine the day.

It is one of my favorite memories.

CHAPTER 80
ali love

After Ali had left—maybe that night, maybe the next day—I looked back at the evening. Saw his pale shoulders again, saw those vulnerable fists at his side, and I knew that was the moment.

I was in love. Another *Truth* moment for me. Silent and solid, with room around the edges for growth.

Being in love with Ali was like breathing underwater, not breathing underwater like drowning, but like having a superpower.

Yes!

Being in love with Ali gave me *superpowers*. I was fully ME when I was with him. And I was never, ever, ever ashamed of crying in front of him.

I'd be watching a movie and weeping and he'd take my hand.

"*Sulugoz* (wet eye)," he'd murmur. "I love it when you cry at movies. It's one of the things I love about you. Your compassion. And sweetness. It's charming."

And then he'd kiss my hand.

A month later, Ali was at my house talking to his ex-wife on the phone. It was nice. Weird. Good. Beautiful.

He paced in the kitchen, telling Pat about me. So sweet. He was nervous. He talked about me, pacing with his wine. We were about to go on a vacation. On Sunday and Monday, we were going to the coast with his friends.

I was so in love. I felt healthy and happy and whole with Ali. I loved his dogs. I loved his voice, his walk, his friends, the way he was with me and Clover and Robert, and about everything.

I loved that he basically lived with me, and I with him, half the time after only a month of dating. I loved that we walked the dogs together and made the bed together.

I loved that he sketched and drew while listening to records. And it made me laugh (to myself, of course) that he lined up things—paperclips, post-it notes, rocks, little trinket boxes—while talking on the phone to his mom or his friend in Wisconsin.

He moved to the bathroom next.

"I'm sorry I didn't tell you about her earlier," I heard him say.

This man was considerate and kind and loyal and honorable. And I loved him.

"What do you like about me?" I asked Ali one night. The kids were at Paul's and Ali was over, lounging on the couch, listening to music.

"Hmmm." He tugged his arm under my neck so that he could pull me closer and kiss the top of my head. "I like that you're a writer." He smoothed my hairline with his lips and warmth fell into me, surprising me a little.

I liked that I was a writer, too. And to have him claim that about me made me proud. Successful somehow. Even though I had published nothing at that point.

"I like ...that you are compassionate and sweet." He kissed my eyebrow. "I like that you have a Ganesh in your house. Because I do, too."

I'd seen it.

"And." He squeezed me tighter. "I liked that when I told you my mom's story on our first date, you teared up. I thought, 'Who is this woman that when she hears about a woman she may never meet, cries for her?' It seemed important to me right then."

I sighed and hugged him back. I never ever worried about rejection with him. I was never *afraid* to be me with him. And that was *truly a first* for me. (*No lie.*)

Did Ali bring out the truth in me? Or was I already telling myself the truth by that time?

Either way, I was a new person with Ali. A renewed me. The enhanced edition. Being in love with Ali was a new, soul-satisfying way of life. It wasn't just that love filled me up in a new way—down to my capillaries. Our relationship allowed me to be the real me, for the first time ever. The changed me.

Or maybe it was the other way around. I had found self-honesty through dancing, maybe had already changed, *and* had painfully recognized a lifetime of lying to myself. Maybe *that* gave my relationship with Ali those special powers. That capillary-filling romantic-sexual-I'm-so-alive love.

Plus, his butt looked amazing in jeans. (*No lie.*)

And his swagger! Oh, my gosh. (*Swoon.*)

(My stepmother and I even giggled about that swagger later, like schoolgirls. But don't tell Ali. He'd be embarrassed.)

CHAPTER 81

missing ali

It was winter, and I was *thinking thinking* too much. But breathing and feeling, too. Soaking up the snuggly dogs next to me on the couch (covered by a sheet to cut down on the doggie hair), relaxing in my nightgown and robe still (it was noon), and enjoying an orange and dancing fire in the wood stove. Also, Urdu music from Atif Aslam. I loved the sound of spoken Urdu/Hindi.

Ali had only been gone for five days. He was visiting his mom in India. She lived there half the year, and since he hadn't seen her in three years (nor India at all), he went.

I'd wanted to visit India for years and years. I had Ganesh statues in almost every room. I burned *puja* often and, until recently, worked in an Indian restaurant for minimum wage just so I could be around the sights, smells, sounds, and culture of India. So, I was glad he was there. And I was also a little sad.

I'd stopped by Ali's house to pick up a couple of things I needed after he left. When I walked in, I had to smile. The house smelled of him, and I inhaled his essence. I saw evidence of me all over. I felt fuzzy and warm, and seeing his home made me think of all the reasons I loved him and was proud of him all over again. We worked together well; we played together well. We got things done, we loved, we cooked, slept, talked, danced, partied, rested, and walked our dogs together. The time we spent in each other's company was divine and pure and exciting and lovely and ... everything I wanted.

So why was I sad? Just because he wasn't there? I knew how to be apart from someone I loved. For months and months. Ali and I would see each other in T-minus sixteen days. He was returning on Christmas. Wasn't that the best Christmas present you could think of? Not that I was really a Christmassy sort of person; I was more into Solstice celebrations. But still. The significance didn't escape me.

Maybe my melancholy was precisely *because* of that past long distance relationship. I was feeling a wee bit triggered without my man there. That was all. Just missing him. I knew that he'd love to be here with his doggies and his love and that fire. Napping. Or reading.

Actually. Probably if he were here right now, we'd be having brunch somewhere that served a Bloody Mary. And then we would walk the dogs in some woodsy or beachy area for a couple of hours.

Heaven.

I was getting to know his dogs—my step-doggies—more and more each day. Casey Jones leaned against me and looked at me with soulful eyes. "When's he coming back?" And Banjo. *Banjito.* He seemed the most unaffected by this short-lived transition.

Humphrey was becoming excessively neurotic on our walks and harder and harder to handle—making the walks WAY shorter than I (or the dogs) wanted them to be.

Casey Jones and Humphrey were growing ... not *fond* of

each other exactly ... but I sometimes caught them licking each other, or wagging at each other. And they would share the couch and the bed with me.

Our little blended family was growing in love with each other, and my kids loved the extra dogginess of our days, too.

CHAPTER 82
sleepovers

By the beginning of the next year, I still hadn't been journaling consistently, even though I knew I was much healthier when I did. Part of my journaling process was the personal check-in, and I didn't feel—yet—that I could do that around Ali. It seemed too personal still. Plus, it was something I mostly did in the mornings and on mornings when I woke up with Ali, I just wanted to stay in bed with him.

But I climbed out of the lovely Ali-warm bed, despite wanting to crawl back into the cocoon of love, his arms wrapped around me. I let the dogs out before I used the bathroom and brushed my teeth. Then, I heated water and tea in a saucepan on the stovetop.

After the dogs were back in and I'd poured myself a mug of chai, Humphrey curled next to me on the couch, and I pulled out my journal. Ali had told me earlier in the week that he didn't think he could live with the children. I wanted to look at that in my journal. Just to see if anything came up.

We lived so close and slept over at each other's home so frequently that we practically lived together, anyway. As I wrote, an awareness seeped out onto the page. Any anxiety that came up in me about Ali not thinking he could live with my kids was just triggered baggage from Nazim. I wasn't lying to myself.

I smiled and put the journal away.

I made another cuppa and one for Ali. He heard me in the kitchen and got up. He hugged me—so warm from the bed—and went to wash his face.

I'm so in love, I whispered while he was in the bathroom.

I loved it when he slept over.

CHAPTER 83

addictions are running amok

It was snowing outside, which, for the Willamette Valley, was usually rare. But global warming had changed our weather patterns permanently, it seemed. Now, there was a summer fire season and a winter storm season in Oregon when there never had been before.

Humphrey stood in front of the fireplace, torn between sitting with me on the couch—which he felt he couldn't do because Casey Jones was already there—and Ali at the table because he had food.

The only reason my wicked dietary and personal habits didn't completely horrify me during the winter was because it was winter. And that sort of behavior only happened in winter.

I didn't use 'it being winter' as an excuse for unhealthy behavior, but a way of *understanding* of how completely off track I became. I seemed to lose the ability to take care of myself properly in the wintertime. I forgot to take my supplements, I bitched about every yoga class on my schedule—and barely made it to one a week, sometimes none—and I ate sugar like it was the last edible thing on the planet.

I also Netflixed.

Yes. I used Netflix as a verb.

Netflix had become almost as addictive as sugar for me. I snuck in episodes of The Paradise, Ms. Fisher's Murder Mysteries, and Boardwalk Express during the day, and watched movies at night with Ali. And on sick days, I watched entire seasons of Downton Abbey. (But that's hardly wrong; fevers must give us an excuse to be a little naughty.)

And addictions to Netflix and sugar—while they could strike at any time—seemed to flare up when my defenses were down.

For instance, if I was tired and overweight because I ate a bunch of sugar and carbs (because it was winter), causing my thyroid disease to spike my hormones to frightening levels, causing me to become *more* tired, so I ate more sugar to get more energy, which caused me to crash, which caused *more* fatigue, and then finally caused depression, I ran straight to Netflix, chocolate chewies from Market of Choice's bakery, and four or five glasses of wine or cider a week.

In my depressive, addictive, "poor me" induced haze, I'd forget to take my Vitamin D and iron supplements I *really, really* needed to function. It was all an annoying, boring, and exhausting cycle.

Each spring it seemed to dissipate, though.

Thank God.

Chronically, February was the worst month for me. But this year, I suspected I'd get an Ali-sized pass. Nothing like new relationship energy to distract from the worst of the winter depression.

Humphrey finally laid down on the floor near the fireplace. Ali joined me on the couch to read, and Alison Krauss played at low volume on the speakers.

CHAPTER 84

ex-wife

One evening, snuggled on his couch, listening to a streaming *Roots Reggae* radio show, Ali asked me if it bothered me that he was still married to his ex-wife. They'd been apart for years but had stayed married, on paper only, so that he could continue to furnish her with health insurance. She was a cancer survivor.

"No. Of course not," I said.

But I wondered.

I checked in. *Was I lying?*

I felt *something* about it. But what? Jealousy? I didn't think so, because Ali had clarified that while he had a compassionate love for a woman he had spent a decade with, he no longer wanted to be in a romantic relationship with her. Ever again. And I believed him. And I trusted him. Even to visit her, which he'd done already.

Besides, *I* was in his arms, his heart. So no, I wasn't jealous of her, but maybe of her title. I snuggled deeper, and he kissed my forehead.

Marriage signified to me a ritual bonding between two

people who loved each other, devoted themselves to each other, and wanted to share their happiness with all of their friends and family. Marriage also signified an element of stability and safety for dreaded emergencies and tragedies.

So, maybe what I was feeling was a little leftover social constraint. Maybe. Maybe not. I certainly didn't think those who didn't marry were "living in sin." But I didn't like my last name anymore. I was still carrying Paul's surname. I knew I could change it legally to whatever I wanted, but I also liked the feeling of belonging with someone. I wanted Ali's name so I could wrap myself up in him. To wear him wherever I went.

CHAPTER 85
depression feels like

If I hadn't felt so healthy, I'd have thought I was coming down with something. Muscle aches, irritability, emotional weakness. And forgetfulness. But, I suspected it was just depression. I didn't want to leave the bed that morning—I just didn't want the day to start. If it started, I knew I'd have to be witty and creative, but I felt gray and mushy.

A therapist once told me it was hard to be a creative person and to choose our life's work, because *all* the things were possible. I *could* be a full-time writer. I *could* start a farm, take sign language lessons, or be a public speaker and travel the world. All those things were possible. It was the choosing that was paralyzing. There were too many options, and they all sounded vitally important and interesting.

I tried to describe my depression to Ali. I told him it was like walking through Jell-O—everything was just so much harder to do.

I found myself staring at the floor or the tablecloths or the stack of books on the side table and not really seeing them. I used to do that when Rob died, and my face crumpled and tears leaked out unwanted. I swallowed them away and reminded myself it was winter. It would pass.

I felt delicate, too, like take-my-arm-and-walk-back-to-the-house-because-I've-walked-too-far delicate. For years, I'd been pining away for 18th century period movies—thinking I'd been born in that era in another life and wishing I lived in that era whenever I felt overwhelmed in my current life circumstances. When I was in high school, I often felt I'd been born in the wrong era.

But recently, it dawned on me I had been pining to be a *gentleman's daughter* in a family rich enough to have servants. I didn't need to live in the 18th century. I just needed to be rich enough to have servants.

I mean, I wasn't pining to be rich, really. Material possessions had never been a driving force for me at all. But I was tired. A lot. And when that happened, I felt weak and in need of assistance. So, yeah. Servants. (*Truth.*)

CHAPTER 86

costa rica

One day, very early into our dating—after making love—I propped myself up on my elbow. "Would you ever consider moving to Costa Rica and living in an intentional community?"

Better to blurt it out. It was still very much on my mind. I wanted to move there and build a house. I wanted to be an expat.

He looked at me and smiled. "Sure."

I hiked myself up farther. "Really?" How could he answer so quickly without discussing it? "Are you serious? Why?" I asked.

"I've always liked the idea of living in an intentional community. Being with like-minded people and treating the land right."

"Huh. Well, that's good." I laid down again. "Because I have land there. And I'd love to move there as soon as the kids are out of high school. They don't want to come with me."

That year, Ali took me to Costa Rica for my birthday, a

grand gesture that I accepted gratefully and, almost, without guilt. It was a pretty big present.

∼

DESPITE MY ASS HURTING FROM SITTING SO MANY HOURS in two days, and my feet swelling up, puffy in my flip-flops, on the bus ride to Palmer Norte, both Ali and I felt that, though we had just arrived and hadn't even reached our destination, we didn't want to leave. A week would not be enough in Costa Rica. It already felt like home.

I once daydreamed about farming our own land, with goats and ducks and bees and plots of gardens, but then Ali and his Wise Words put me in my place. His frankness and wisdom stopped me dead in my tracks.

"Look at your yard, Valerie," he said. "We can't even handle that. What makes you think we can run a *farm* in Costa Rica?"

"Oh, all right. But can we still do yoga in the mornings after making love at sunrise?"

I loved showing him Costa Rica. He loved the location, the mountain breezes, the warm water at the beaches, the surf culture--"*Maybe I'll take up surfing when we move here*"--the permaculture, and the *Cerveza*.

We easily made friends with our "neighbors" on the mountain and picked out the lot we wanted and the trees we wanted to plant on the lot. We visited the gardens and deliberately walked by the canopy tour zip line. I'd already done it once. Never again. *Shudder*.

I turned thirty-nine years old in Costa Rica. I woke very early to a quiet radio playing somewhere. I thought it was my alarm clock, waking me for morning yoga, but then knew it wasn't. Birds twittered and called outside. I listened for howler monkeys. Instead, a lone hammer and drill. Construction. It actually wasn't an unpleasant sound. It wasn't the sound of a Walmart being built. More like four guys building a deck or something. And with an off-in-the-distance sound to it. It was quieter than Ali breathing next to me, doing that comforting, almost-snoring thing.

The overhead fan ruffled the curtains in the window. Ali stirred beside me. I glanced over and moved my leg to touch his, reassuring.

"Happy birthday," Ali murmured with his eyes closed. He promptly fell back asleep.

I grinned. I got up and peed, closed the bedroom windows and door, and lay back down with an eye mask to block out the sunlight coming from around the four sides of both blackout shades. The equatorial sun rises early there.

I snuggled into bed, wondering at the two opposing facts that were both true and certain at the same time. One, I was a little shivery for the first time in twenty-four hours, so I pulled up the sheet half-covering me to guard against the ceiling fan's breeze. Two, I was still sticky. Tacky. Like a layer of glue stuck to my skin, almost dried. Strange that both were accurate.

I rested under the mask and the ceiling fan, and twenty minutes later, the construction sounds stopped. I tried to sleep again. Community yoga wasn't for another hour and a half. But no.

The jungle birds, the soft morning light, and the thought of fresh coffee beckoned. I wanted to putter in the morning without worrying about Ali being bored, waiting around for me. And I wanted to write.

So, I did what any other self-respecting woman on her birthday on vacation in a foreign country did. I stayed in bed and journaled instead. And then snuggled my honey, eyes closed, for thirteen minutes until the alarm went off.

~

ONE MORNING THERE, WE TOOK A DIP IN THE POOL AND then walked over to an animal sanctuary. Later, I made breakfast with fruits, veggies, and eggs from the community farm and gardens. We drank fresh guava juice that our neighbor, Lisa, and I had made from guavas we'd picked the day before.

The next day, after breakfast at the community center, we did our laundry and packed up. We hiked down to a waterfall on the property to do a releasing ceremony in the river water. We would leave the following day.

During our trip, Ali said promising things that lightened my heart.

"When we move here ..."
"We should look into ..."
"When we come back ..."
"We should learn Spanish together."
"I don't want to leave."

~

I HATED LEAVING.

When we returned to Oregon, Ali held my hand tight.

"I'm grieving my relationship with Pat. That it's really ending. I know it, because I'm falling deeper in love with you and making plans for my future. My future with you."

Swoon.

CHAPTER 87

cuthbert acid trip

Sharing an acid trip is personal, on many levels. Especially one with some distance behind it. It's been many years since the *Further* show at the Cuthbert Amphitheater, and I don't recall the nuances of my time under the influence of LSD.

What I can tell you is that it changed me. Helped me to move from one stuck area to a more expansive place.

I was one thing before, and another after.

Which was often the case with acid.

Which was why people took it. It was a medicine, of sorts. New (and old) studies have shown that micro-dosing helped with a whole slew of mental, emotional, and psychological issues, from PTSD to quitting smoking.

On that occurrence, that trip, I learned to trust Ali.

Not that I didn't trust him before, but our relationship (in *my* mind, anyway) went to a new level of trust.

I mostly could feel in control of my body and mind and surroundings that night. But, increasingly, I found I wouldn't be able to get home on my own, given the state I was in. And, for some clouded reason, I was fearful of this. Shaken.

I knew I could call for a taxi, but the thought of consciously finding the phone number and talking to a stranger and communicating where I lived was a quest I just didn't have in me.

I was trapped there, and that sharp and pointy realization felt glaring and harsh.

"I don't know how I'm going to get home," I said to Ali.

"Don't worry, babe. I'll get you home."

"But I can't drive. And you can't drive."

"That's okay. I'll be fine by the time we need to leave." He squeezed my hand. "And if not, we'll take a taxi home."

"What about the car?"

"We'll come back and get it tomorrow. I'm sure they are used to cars staying in the parking lot overnight."

I think we had this same exact conversation, almost verbatim, three more times that night—until I let go.

I let go of being in control. It clicked, like the clarity on the meadow that one day during my text conversation with Nazim, *I could trust Ali to take care of me.* I could put my life in his hands, and he would be brave when I couldn't. He would guide me when I needed direction. I could trust him. Period. In all things.

I wept with relief and understanding and giddiness. And love.

I knew I'd made it through another level of trust and depth with Ali.

I was euphoric. I relaxed into the rest of evening and danced and walked and looked and saw and danced some more.

Before that night, I felt confident that I'd gotten Truth

down. Honesty with myself was easier and easier, but sometimes it seemed to come out defensive.

Here! My truth! Take it if you can stand it! Are you strong enough? And after Cuthbert, I could soften into trust, knowing Ali would be gentle with my Truth and honor it.

He was a rock. He could stand it. He could stand Me.

And I reveled in the newness of that.

CHAPTER 88
things i loved about ali

- He was a good man.
- He was fair.
- He smiled.
- He loved with his whole heart.
- He was attentive.
- He laughed and liked ridiculous things.
- He loved my body.
- He loved *Me*.
- When he was sick or in pain, he wasn't mean.
- He liked art and music.
- He was a writer and a printmaker.
- He danced.
- He fit me—physically, emotionally, sexually.
- I liked myself when I was with him.
- He was an experiencer and a reader.
- He sketched and drew while listening to records, and he lined up little trinkets while talking on the phone.
- He loved dogs.

CHAPTER 89

home life

Casey Jones frantically licked Banjo's ear, and then nonchalantly wandered off. Ali refilled the doggies' water bowl and put on one of his favorite sweaters. One that could uphold the dog hair from the couch a little better than his work sweaters. But he moved to the kitchen table with me and Robert to eat his breakfast, and it didn't matter.

As of late, I felt artistically blocked. I would have a brief urge to draw or write, and I'd ignore it, so then my soul and creative chakra would shrivel a little, like a neglected and ignored child. I needed to make time for creativity. I had to. It helped me breathe, and it kept the depression away.

I wanted to write poetry. To garden, to clean out my kitchen cupboards. To write my bio and promotional brochure for the massage clients I would now be seeing. No more waitressing or working for others. I was starting my own massage business, and my new office was in my favorite yoga studio. Built-in clients!

I finished eating and gathered my plate and Robert's—

he'd already moved on to playing video games on his laptop, which I allowed once he was ready for school. I put the dishes in the sink and started the water to boil for another cup of tea.

"I love you," Robert said.

"I love you, too," I said.

"...both of you," Robert amended.

I literally did a double-take, like in cartoons, and looked over at Ali. My eyes widened and my mouth dropped open.

Ali's face registered a mixture of his own disbelief, but also a bit of delight.

"I love you, too," Ali said.

Nobody said anything else. Later, I took Robert and Clover to school, and Ali went to work. But, boy, oh boy. I felt elated and stunned for the rest of the day. A far cry from a little boy kicking his feet and exclaiming I shouldn't have a man in my bed unless Paul was dead.

My friend Deanna bought too much compost. Ali and I spent weeks bagging up the extra stuff at her house and bringing it to my garden. We stirred it and straw into the soil, dug trenches around each raised bed area, trimmed an already overgrown section of the garden that I called the container garden, laid straw down in between the beds and around the cherry tree to discourage weeds, weeded the raspberry canes, and put up the rest of the garden fencing so the dogs couldn't get in and dig up stuff.

I finally transplanted the local starts I'd been accumulating. Sixteen strawberry plants, three pepper plants, a cherry tomato plant for Ali—I don't like tomatoes, raw ones anyway—and one lavender plant to replace the one that mysteriously died. Ali cleared some blackberry vines behind the shed, too. I needed to fertilize the blueberries next.

Robert, after being forced to help in the garden a wee bit on Saturday—truly, it took him longer to find socks and put them on than the time he helped—asked why we were having a garden.

Had I forgotten to talk about sustainability with him?

"So we can eat," I said.

"What? We're not eating anything else, but what grows here? No meat?!" He was getting frantic.

"Well," I said patiently, "not everything. We'll still buy meat and things we don't grow at the Farmers' Market."

"Oh." His shoulders slumped down and he took a breath. "Whew. I need meat."

CHAPTER 90

dark moment

Tamara came over one sunny winter's day. She was missing her long-distance boyfriend. (I didn't dare tell her not to bother. That it wouldn't work. She'd seen me with Nazim. She knew the pros and cons, the ups and downs.)

She flopped on my bed and took a selfie, then texted it to her guy. She tried one with sunglasses next. Each photo got more provocative until she thought it would be hot if there was a picture of me and her kissing.

I obliged for fun.

Memory is a funny thing. Researchers and scientists say that every time someone pulled out a memory to examine it, it changed. Which makes memoir writing tricky.

My journal entry from that day said that the kiss escalated a teeny bit, but then stopped almost immediately. I didn't remember the escalation. Still don't. I just remembered that we did it as a joke, of sorts. For shock value, more than anything.

In full disclosure—because honesty was uber-important to both of us—I told Ali about the kiss. Over the phone.

He got real quiet.

"Maybe we shouldn't do this then," Ali said.

This.

He meant Us.

"What? No, Ali. Please. No."

Panic.

Red alert. Red alert.

Danger. Danger.

I couldn't see for the neon flashing signs in my brain.

How could I make him change his mind? Was it made up already? In that split second of honesty? Had I been wrong all along? Been wrong to vow truthfulness when that was where it would lead?

I was already in love with Ali. That was the truth—though I hadn't told him yet.

I could hear in his voice, in that one statement—*Maybe we shouldn't do this then*—that he was worried and triggered, baggage from two major relationships before me.

Shit!

Did I ruin it? Us? My stomach roiled. My hands sweated around the phone so much I had to wipe the purple case on my pants when I hung up.

Whatever I fumbled out after that gave him enough pause, and he agreed to meet me for dinner at Chao Pra Ya later that night.

What if he said it wasn't going to work out? What if he said I had lost his trust? I was frantic. Jittery.

Why did I even say anything about the kiss in the first place? It meant nothing. It was a *joke.*

But I was truthful now. I didn't lie.

Telling the truth was the only way forward; otherwise, I'd be stuck in another Paul/Nazim relationship, lying to myself about how I felt and who I was and what I needed and wanted.

Even if telling the truth meant losing right now, it didn't mean losing forever, and it certainly didn't mean that I wouldn't find the Perfect Love, if this didn't turn out to be that.

If I told the truth and Ali rejected me because of it, then he wasn't my perfect love, anyway.

To this day, when I think of that time, the back of my throat sours like I'm about to throw up.

CHAPTER 91

the key

That night at Chao Pra Ya—a Thai food restaurant in The Whit—Ali and I sat at a table for two in the middle of the room, next to a partition. I was nervous. I don't remember what I was wearing. I don't remember what I did with my hair. I don't even remember what I said exactly. I only remember the sickness. The dread.

Ali was perfect for me. It was true. We matched. How could I lose him before it even really started? I knew it was fast, but I loved him already. He just didn't know it yet. Or maybe he did. Maybe that was the night I told him.

Isn't it funny which things we remember and which we don't? I always thought that the important things stuck with you. But they don't. Not really. I can't remember what Rob's laugh sounded like. I can't remember which of my kids made me the bead necklace I saved for over ten years. I can't remember when my sister Carrie last spoke to me. And I can't remember which arm my son broke when he was in first grade. (He says it was the right, but I think it was the left.)

I don't remember when I told Ali that I loved him. And I

don't remember him saying it back to me. But I *do* remember, at Chao Pra Ya, that I gave Ali a little box. In my mind, it was a little golden paper box, but it could've been black.

He looked delighted at the prospect of a present.

He opened it.

I watched his face.

"Is this ..."

"It's a key to my house," I said.

He smiled.

"I know it's a bit early for that, but ..."

"Did you have this made today? Just for me?" he asked.

My heart dipped. I so wanted that to have been the truth. But it wasn't. In an attempt to prove my devotion and love, I had thought of giving him the key. Proof of my seriousness. An apology, of sorts. An admittance of my wretchedness for casting my character into doubt. An invitation—to join me in love and growth together. A plea. *Don't give up on me yet.*

I had an extra key to the house, and I rummaged around in the kitchen drawer until I found it. It was blue, with a *fleur-de-lis* on it. I wiped it clean, nestled it in cotton, and tied a bow around the box, hoping and praying it would be enough to start our life together. To start our love together.

I could've lied. It was what he wanted to hear. *Yes. I made it just for you.* But I'd promised. I'd promised myself. No more lies. And I'd promised him. *I'll never lie to you.*

If I lied, I'd make him happy for a moment, but he wouldn't recover from the betrayal. Somehow, I knew this wouldn't be a little lie. It was important. I couldn't start off our relationship with a lie, and it would be entrapment, because maybe he'd only stay with me because of the key. Only because I'd made a key specifically for him. (Which I hadn't.)

But I couldn't lie. (*Truth.*) It stuck in my throat. That lie. Instead, my hands tremored under the skin and my heart raced.

What if this is the end? What if I said no, and he was so disappointed he couldn't recover from the Tamara kiss? The kiss that meant nothing. Just a joke.

If the pretend kiss ended Ali and I and telling the truth about the key—that I just found it and didn't make it specifically for him—sealed that ending, would I ever have the conviction to be honest about what mattered at another time?

I certainly hoped that I would. Because I was done with lying. (*Truth*.)

"No," I admitted. "I had it already, but I wanted you to have it."

Here I am. I'm worthwhile, in love with you, and want to grow with you. This is my truth.

He smiled and put the lid back on the box, setting it near his glass. I breathed easier past the sharp, jagged fear of losing him.

I'd told the truth.

He picked up his menu, glanced at the box, and smiled again.

I had to tell the truth. I didn't want to lie to myself or anyone else ever again. And Ali and I had promised each other honesty.

It was really all he'd ever asked of me.

CHAPTER 92

crazy mom writer

I'm a voyeuristic writer. I've always wanted to know what other writers' days look like, how they actually fit all the things into their life, convinced that somehow I was doing everything wrong. Because I often paid little attention to what I did in the course of a given day, out of that same voyeuristic curiosity, one day I cataloged my own Writer's Day.

- Alarm rang at 6:10 a.m.; hit snooze twice.
- Let dogs out; woke son for school.
- Showered and dressed.
- Fed dogs.
- Made lunches for three people.
- Checked the garden to see if it needed water.
- Made myself tea and toast; checked emails.
- Drove my son to school, then went to a coffee shop to meet a friend for a chat.
- Read a couple of blog posts and articles; re-posted them on my author social media sites.

- Opened up Scrivener files and wrote on novel manuscript while I waited for my friend—1,000 new words!
- Visited with my friend for an hour.
- Went home and snacked; read a magazine article and Facebooked a *teeny* bit. (*Honest!*)
- Worked on a manuscript review for a client for two hours.
- Picked up my son and his friend from school.
- Stopped at the farmers' market on the way home and picked up my raw juice order.
- When home, called the vet because one dog ate my vitamins and supplements that I'd set out to take that morning, and forgot.
- Vacuumed all the floors in the house—except my children's. You just don't go in there.
- Took a ten-minute break with wine.
- Greeted oldest child fresh home from school and watched them perform a dance routine they are learning at school.
- Lead son and his friend in a snack-finding mission.
- Unloaded and reloaded the dishwasher and wiped down the counters.
- Fed the dogs.
- Started dinner.
- Texted with a friend, trying to get a group of us to go to the movies that night.
- Watched oldest child again (different dance routine section)
- Aided oldest child in snack mission.
- Checked on dinner.
- Started baking bread in the bread machine.

- Contemplated mopping the muddy dog prints off the solid surface floors but yearned for the hot tub long enough that the urge to clean mostly passed.
- Swept the carport instead, and took out all the trash.
- Wondered if I should clean off the dining room table, but—it being 6:00 p.m.—decided I was too tired for anything boring like that and yearned for Netflix and Hulu alternatives.
- Remembered the hot tub ... and then that I was taking my oldest to a play a student friend was performing in, and that I still intended to henna my hair that night. Nix on the hot tub.
- Drank more wine in hopes of an evening plan forming.
- Acknowledged the Swiss chard still needed to be prepped for dinner and silently whined to myself. I took another sip of whine—I mean wine.
- Craved chocolate; had a small can of peaches instead.
- Craved chocolate and ate two handfuls of chocolate sprinkles out of the baking cupboard.
- Noted that this was all because I *wanted to get in the hot tub*, but couldn't yet—hot tubbing requiring nudity, and nudity and driving my kid to the Wildish Theater didn't mix.
- Checked the chicken and rice again.
- Tried to find a game for the younger teens to play. They ignored me and listened to weird military cadences on their smart phones. They gave the Wii a try.
- I pulled the chocolate sprinkles out of the cupboard because I hadn't actually eaten them yet, just

written about it because it seemed like something I'd do. Recognized that since I hadn't actually eaten them, I could still make the healthy choice *not* to eat them. Told myself that since I'd already written I *had*, I needed to be true to the original sentiment of the daily entry. So, I ate them. (*That's impeccability of word for you. Isn't that one of the Four Agreements?*)

- One dog looked at me as if asking to go outside; I remembered about the chard again. I didn't want to make it. None of the kids would eat it, I was sure. Did I want to make it just for myself?
- I let the dogs out.
- I went on a hunt for batteries so the boys could both play with the Wii.
- Closed the back door. Remembered my propensity for locking dogs outside and checked the house to make sure all three were inside.
- I marveled at the teens all talking and hanging out together without freaking out and smiled at my 14-year-old's deep voice, then worried if he said "bitch" to his video games too much.
- Checked the dinner again. It was done.
- Decided it was too late to make the chard. Felt lowly and guilty for not eating my healthy greens and hoped that my *healthier* partner wouldn't find out that I'd ditched my veggies out of laziness again.
- Informed the kids that dinner was ready and convinced myself that I'd fulfilled my parenting duties for the day and I could be done. *Woo Hoo!*
- Closed the back door because somehow it was open again.

- Checked the house for all three dogs again. One was missing. I let him in. He was looking in the living room window for me.
- Ate dinner while watching the last half of a *West Wing* episode I'd already started.
- Dropped off my oldest at the play.
- Knew that this would be a perfect time to henna my hair but wanted to watch another episode first.
- Craved chocolate again, so I shifted from wine to hot chocolate with marshmallows.
- Watched two episodes of West Wing waiting for my kid to text me they were done with the play.
- Washed dinner dishes and wiped counters again.
- Changed t.p. roll in the bathroom and took recycling out.
- Hennaed hair.
- Picked up oldest from the theater.
- Sat in the hot tub.
- Showered to wash the henna out.
- Went to pick up partner at the airport at midnight.
- We visited a little, then brushed our teeth and went to sleep.

My day pleased me. It really was one of my favorites. Probably because it was so well balanced. It was long, and I didn't sit down much—except for the West Wing part—but most of the aspects of my life were lovingly attended to.

I created new words for my book. I socialized. I worked on client work. I hung out with my awesome kids. I cleaned and cooked, looked after my dogs and garden, and still had time for personal grooming and relaxing. It was great. Here's hoping I re-create that type of balance in future days. [*sound of wine glass clinking with a hot chocolate mug*]

CHAPTER 93
houseboat adventures

In the baked heat of August, just before our one-year anniversary in 2013, Ali and I stayed on a houseboat at Cove Palisades State Park with a bunch of Ali's friends, who were now my friends.

Someone untethered the two house boats and started the engine. We explored the rock formations and watched birds and clouds. We water-skied, shared delicious food, smiled at each other, rested, napped in the sun, and found beauty in all the colors and textures.

"It's so wild that I can feel connected to the beauty and power of Mother Earth, and the expansiveness of Everything," Ali said. "Being a part of something vibrant and living, and then—"

He took my hand.

"—feel the sheer largeness of it all—the insignificance of me within it all." He shook his head and stared at the sunset.

"We're just sharing a human experience with each other. You know?" he said. "And hopefully learning along the way." He nodded to himself and sipped his beer.

Throughout that first night on the boat, Ali repeatedly hugged me in great squeezes, and love rippled through me in alternating waves of euphoria and contentment.

We lay down on the roof of the houseboat to watch the stars and Perseid meteor showers. We held each other and kissed and played under the covers. And then he said it.

"I want to marry you," he whispered.

My heart swelled and thudded under my sternum. Breathless with the sky's depth and color, tears rushed to my eyes and leaked out the corners.

"I want to marry you, too," I said. (*No fucking lie.*)

He said we should give each other names when we got married. Ones that represented all that the other meant to us. That sounded hard. Just one word? Like a nickname with an agenda, albeit a romantic one.

He sang to me in Turkish out on that boat.

CHAPTER 94

my favorite house

I lit incense for the first time in ages. I took off my slippers and covered my head before lighting the stick, just like I did when I worked in the Indian restaurant. I waved the ember in front of Ganesh's statue, touched his forehead, touched mine, and then touched my heart chakra. I walked around the house, waving the incense stick at corners and doorways and windows.

Then, I bowed to the Ganesh by the front door three times and finished my circuit back to the kitchen window where I started. I put the incense in its holder, lowered the wool shawl from my head, and slipped my slippers back on.

I made myself some blackberry sage tea with honey, sank into the squishy green couch next to Humphrey, and began pulling the loose threads of a blog post idea out of my head. I used to do this morning ritual every morning, and I missed it.

Ali and I had been dating for close to one year. Our relationship was lovely and warm and beautiful. Easy from the start. I was grateful that he'd given me a second chance to prove my love for him, to prove my worth—and so glad I had grown up enough to be with Ali.

CHAPTER 95

marriage trigger

I sat in the sun at my back door. Humphrey was wandering the backyard grasses and sniffing. He was so much happier alone without the other dogs there. (Or was it just Casey Jones he was anxious around?)

It was warmer outside than inside because the sun warmed my clothes. I soaked up the Vitamin D. I was feeling a little melancholy about the house. I really liked it, despite a couple of unsavory things, like the bathroom size and that the location of the back door in my bedroom.

But I loved the location, the neighborhood, the proximity to a field Humphrey could run in if I was careful, and the yard was perfection. I had so many visions for it.

I wanted Ali to move there. I wanted to buy that house, because I liked it, and it was inexpensive and would serve as income for us when we were in Costa Rica. It was also a place we could always call home when we found ourselves in Eugene, temporarily or permanently. The only fly in the ointment was that Ali didn't like it. He liked *his* place, but it was too small for us.

This place was too small for us, too, when I considered three large dogs being here—with too many tight spaces for Casey Jones and Humphrey to get into grumbles over.

But I still brought it up. I told Ali I wanted him to move in. He didn't respond the way I thought he would.

"I love you," he said. "We basically live together five days a week, but I like my alone time and I just don't want to live with the kids. I hope that's okay."

Hours later, I approached the subject again. "I spent two years trying to get Nazim to marry me so we could live together, and four years trying to get Paul to marry me, and five to get him to pay attention to me. I'm starting to feel unworthy." My voice cracked.

"I'm not Paul. And I'm definitely not Nazim." He pulled me to his chest.

I sniffled and snuggled in and cried a little.

"We'll get married," he said. Then he snorted. "I just have to get divorced first."

We laughed at the same time.

Ali was a good man.

CHAPTER 96

moving again

My landlord wanted to sell the house I lived in, but I didn't qualify for a home loan. Ali didn't want to buy my place because it wasn't big enough for all of us. So, either I had to look for another rental that would move us farther apart—it was great having him within walking distance—or we had to find a rental big enough for all of us to move in to.

Somehow, it made more sense for us to buy a house together instead.

Despite not having had plans to move in together for at least another year, and Ali's concerns about living with the kids, we suddenly were doing that very thing.

Moving in together would mean big changes for all of us, but mostly not-so-big changes. While Ali liked and genuinely cared for and worried about my teenage children, he'd never lived with kids before. I was worried that occasionally he'd need a quiet place to time-out in (not so much different from traditional parents, actually), away from the noise, chaos, and drama teenagers sometimes brought—depending on the kid. I was sure Ali worried a little about that, too.

Our three large dogs and my desire to garden and raise chickens created some unique (but not strange) housing needs. We were obviously looking for a large fenced lot. And we'd need a certain amount of separation of space in the actual living quarters, not to mention the general square footage required for four people, three dogs, lots of art, and a myriad of books.

In our preliminary searching, we found one property in particular that we kept using as a reference. *Do we like this house as much as the other one?* No? Strike it from the list.

As with every home, even "dream ones" you construct yourself, there were things about it that weren't quite perfect. You'd change them if you could. But the positives far out-weighed the bad, and that was the case for this "reference" house we'd found.

The backyard wasn't flat, the location of the home wasn't in my favorite neighborhood, and one bathroom would rarely be used—given its location in the house. Which just seemed wasteful. Other than that, though, it was nearly perfect for our needs. The property taxes were lower than in some places. The dogs wouldn't bottleneck in the hallways. There was a great place for Ali to escape to, *and* it boasted an artist's studio. With at least three artists in the family, that would be great fun to have.

In lean times, if I couldn't manage my rent downtown, I *could* use the studio as a place to practice massage out of. The studio had an outside entrance, and an accessible bathroom—one that wouldn't have clients traipsing through my dog-haired living room, or messy kitchen. Pretty nearly perfect.

We put an offer on it. They accepted. We'd move in the summer.

CHAPTER 97

no wedding ring

Ali told me, out of the blue, that he wouldn't wear a wedding ring. We were having dinner at Hot Mama's Wings. I must have looked stricken.

"Why not?"

He quickly amended his statement.

"Not unless I really, really like it. And I'd have to pick it out. I just don't like the feel of rings on my hands. But I guess I could get used to it if I liked it. And it would have to be silver, or white gold."

I ate a French fry. "Why did you bring that up?"

He wiggled in his seat a little. "I don't know."

He looked a little confused. Caught unawares.

"There was a connection in my brain when I started talking, but I'd forgotten it by the time we came to the end of the discussion." He blinked.

And I had to laugh. It was too bizarre.

We both laughed, and Ali shook his head.

CHAPTER 98

travel: the anti-quest

It was that time in our relationship where I would *Meet the Mom.*

Early in 2015, I went to India with Ali and met his mom for the first time. I was both terrified and thrilled.

Visiting India had been on my wish list for years, even *before* Ali. I once had a plastic bucket in my bedroom labeled INDIA, where I put my waitressing tips. Mostly, I lived off those tips and dipped into the bucket to buy food, so I never got to go. I buzzed with excitement in the months leading up to our vacation.

After we arrived and made our way through the lines, through customs, paperwork, and exchanging money, we pulled our suitcases out into the sticky air. Temporary waist-high metal partitions formed a large semi-octagon around the exit, shielding the disembarking travelers from the waiting public.

We scanned the crowd, and there she was. We waved.

I felt nervous. *What should I call her? Should I kiss her hand like Ali did as a child for his grandfather? Should I touch her feet? No. That was Indian, not Turkish.* (But we were in India!) And here she was, in an Indian dress, with her Indian friend, Bina.

Ali leaned over the partition.

"*Merhaba annem. N'aber güzellik?*" He kissed her cheeks. "And this is Valerie," he said, smiling, proud, travel-worn.

Should I kiss her? I leaned over and offered a hug. She grasped me firmly, and I instantly felt her love. I shook Bina's hand, which morphed into an awkward half-hug.

Fatma, whom I later called *anne* (mom), and her friend, Bina, led us to an opening in the partition, and we followed them to a car. Our driver took us to a marvelous old hotel that used to be luxurious.

I started taking pictures immediately. Some people go on trips to find themselves or to have mystical experiences. I went to India with no such quest. I just wanted to *experience*. Experience anything.

Ali devoured the travel guidebook. He picked out the places he wanted to see. He planned. He memorized names of cities and temples. I, *for the first time in my life*, did not.

Instead, I received. I followed. I looked. What I saw was what I came for: India—Land of Bright Colors, Banyan Trees, and Street Dogs.

Cows, goats and dogs slept in the middle of the road and ate everything—even trash (maybe especially trash). On one drive, I saw fireworks, a wedding procession, and goats peeing all at the same intersection, at the same time. Later that day, there was a parade in the street with music. The reason? Someone old had died, and they were happy—celebrating a long life.

There were many shepherds on the roads there, too. Herding goats or hanging out with their cows while the animals ate the roadside or field grass. Ambulance drivers stopped and peed on the side of the road when not dealing with emergencies.

Along with the dogs and goats, the streets teemed with rickshaws, scooters, bicycles, people, vendors, and trash—right alongside the cars. Cars were actually the minority, with—I'd say—only about a third of the road. Exhaust was everywhere.

Scooters carried everything—jars for water, wood stacks, or up to four people at a time—*including infants*. Indians rarely observed stop signs. Horn signals allowed other drivers, cyclists, walkers, and animals to know a vehicle was coming and to get out of the way. People drove their scooters on major highways and small city streets without shoes, helmet, or protective clothing—just naked feet and *lungis* (a sarong worn by men), a shirt, and perhaps a scarf or earmuffs.

We either walked or took rickshaws to most of our destinations. The only taxis we rode in were to and from airports with our luggage or for day trips to faraway temples.

I had little culture shock at all. Thanks to Nazim, I knew how to use a squat toilet, and I faced one first thing off the plane in the Chennai airport. *And* with no paper. I was fairly adept at the squatting part, and thanks to the education of my ex-boyfriend, I didn't pee on my clothes one bit. It was the water part I was still clumsy with. But no matter. I learned to take napkins and toilet paper with me in my pockets or bag whenever I left our hotel.

The next time I go to India, I'll also take those little bottles of travel hand sanitizer I can pass through security checks with at airports. If the toilets had running water to wash my hands with after pooping in a hole in the ground, there usually wasn't any soap.

I'm not a germaphobe, but when I managed to get poop on my hand while trying to handle cleaning myself with water at a squat toilet in a salwar kameez with no toilet paper—even though I miraculously found two small and partially used napkins in my purse with only marginal amounts of curry stains on them—and then found no soap at the hand-washing station, I knew it was time for some *hand sanitizer*.

It *thrilled* me to find, an hour later, that our lunch destination had soap *and* running water. Even after washing my hands twice, my middle-class, white-girl, North American heebie-jeebies forbade me to eat the South Indian way—with my hands. I was quite adept at it and even impressed a few locals. But that meal had me using a fork. *Lemme tell ya.*

I rarely wore perfume, but there were a couple of times while passing a polluted river or an especially pungent pile of trash when I was grateful to hold a lightly scented *dupatta* (large scarf or shawl) or handkerchief to my nose.

I didn't need to adjust to the food, the heat (I regularly did yoga in a 104-degree heated room), the music, or most of the culture. I knew that when speaking to police, taxi drivers, or restaurant hosts, that they'd look instead to my white male companion.

I knew to look down after making eye contact with a man. I knew beggars would accost me everywhere. I knew rickshaw drivers would charge us double (or more) the going rate. Ali's mom, having lived off and on in India for five years and had been visiting it for thirty, told us to always insist on the use of their meter. If they said "No" or "It's broken," we should walk away and go to the next one. We wouldn't have to walk far.

Driving was definitely only for the locals. There were rules, a rhythm, and a horn language completely un-learnable to anyone else not growing up there. In fact, that was the only culture shock I experienced in India. And it wasn't so much shock as fear.

By my North American standards, Indians drove recklessly, too fast, rudely, and dangerously. Mostly, I reminded myself there was a system to the driving, and as a foreigner, I just had to let go of any fear of road death. It helped to close my eyes.

After about four days of straight, all-day-long sight-seeing, I had headaches from clenching my jaws (a by-product of some of those drives, and the constant interruptions of beggars, street vendors, would-be guides, and rickshaw drivers trying to take us somewhere). My body was sore everywhere, and my feet swelled with the extra walking on uneven ground. I clearly hadn't paced myself.

I gave myself twenty-four hours to recover with room service, feet up in bed, an English-speaking movie on the hotel TV, and an early bedtime. Ali and I lounged the next morning with books and shortened our excursions from that point on to one or two sights per day.

Halfway through our travels, we flew to Pune—where Ali's mother had an apartment—and we stayed with her, slowing our travel and sight-seeing pace even more. A welcome respite for a book lover like me. I read four books in thirteen days and still took a walk every day, saw the OSHO meditation gardens, watched two movies at the Indian cinemas (pretty posh), went to a Parvati temple, visited friends of the family, shopped for *sari* and *salwar kameez* fabrics, got measured for said clothing to be sewn at the tailor's, had a couple of *chappals* (sandals) fixed, and took many rickshaw rides.

Did I learn about myself on this anti-quest? Not especially. Except that maybe I *could* let go and just let others be in charge. I just followed.

Sure. Whatever. I'm just here to experience became my travel motto.

Going to India wasn't just for the guru-inspired. I didn't need a quest to travel to another continent and have an elephant eat flowers out of my hair. I just went and soaked up my surroundings. Heard different languages spoken and listened to streets coming awake. Stepped out of the ordinary and walked on a beach littered with human feces. I even cleansed myself of all my sins in the town of Rameshwaram in the twenty-two wells at the Ramanathaswamy Temple and accidentally got married. (*Truth.*)

CHAPTER 99
accidental marriage

I didn't know what men did at the Ramanathaswamy Temple, but women went in with a new sari on. Ali's mom gifted me one to wear. It was red with thin gold stripes along the edging and the *pallu*, the end you throw over your shoulder.

Then, without our shoes—because we were in a temple—we followed a man who may have been a guide or a Hindu priest through the large meandering temple and stopped at each well.

There was a story to each well. Usually a man of importance, or someone associated with the Hindu mythology, ridded himself of a curse or was absolved of sin at one particular well, or attained wisdom, reached heaven, or received knowledge of past, present, and future at another.

At one well, I could receive the goddess Lakshmi's blessings and at another, I could prevent myself from going to hell.

The idea was to bathe in each of the holy waters at each well—by one of these temple men ladling well water over my head—so that, in the end, I would be absolved of all my sins.

I'd also be completely drenched and take off the wet sari, change into the dry clothes I'd brought with me, and leave the new sari in the changing area. The staff would then collect the saris and distribute them to a local charity.

As I loved ritual, especially as it pertained to sacred things, I was totally game for all of it. Ali's mom and her travel companion did it with me, too—but without the new sari part. Bathers could choose to wear their own clothes home.

Ali followed along and took pictures, but didn't prefer the holy drenching. Apparently, he was fine with his sin, thank you very much.

After I was suitably sin-free, Ali and I approached yet another temple area and were marked with *tikkas* of *vibhuti* ash and red *kumkum* powder on our foreheads.

The *pandit* (Hindu priest) chanted a bit and then asked if we were married. We smiled and looked at each other.

"Not yet," I said.

He chanted some more, then handed Ali a garland of marigolds and instructed him to place it over my head. Which he did.

I was to reciprocate, so I took off the garland and put it over Ali's head.

"Now touch his feet," the man said.

I touched Ali's feet in suitable reverence.

"Now together, put the garland over your mother and both touch her feet," he said.

We did, completely charmed. Ali's mom, Ali, and I all smiled together. It was fun and warm and ritualistic. *And I was in India.* This was by far the coolest thing I'd done in India, maybe in my life.

"And now," the man said, "you are married."

"What?" We both said it in unison.

"For the next seven lifetimes," the *pandit* added.

. . .

After I'd changed into dry clothes and looked at the pile of saris left behind, I decided that one more wouldn't mean much to the poor and I sentimentally kept it for myself. Fatma had gifted it to me—my first gift from Ali's mom.

And, after all, I'd been married in it.

CHAPTER 100

wedding vows

Two and a half years later, we had a party. A three-day wedding extravaganza involving a *mehndi* ceremony, renting out a whole nature resort, and arranging two bands. And we wrote our own vows.

Our friend, Amos, smudged each guest arriving to the meadow with sage—wafting the fragrance with a large feather and purifying the energy that entered our ceremony. Our Country Fair friend, John, played his trumpet for my procession.

My dad walked me to the edge of the field, in front of our guests, and handed me off to Ali. At the altar—Ganesh center stage, of course—our friend and officiant, Kim, lit a beeswax candle, and my dad picked up a clay water pitcher. He poured McKenzie River water over our clasped hands before sitting down.

"Hello, beautiful people," Kim said. "Welcome. Let us ground ourselves today by closing our eyes, and with a hand on our hearts, we'll take three deep breaths."

Peace and love filled my soul, and the jitteriness subsided for a moment.

"There are so many beautiful things in life. This setting, the trees, the creek behind me, the breeze we feel right now. The lovely people here, all the fantastic things we get to experience in this world, to embrace and hold *and love*. And I would suggest that love is the most important part of that equation.

"If we take love out, it becomes a kind of bleak place. A kind of mechanical, automated place."

A baby cried in the audience and someone murmured, "Sorry."

"We love children," Kim said. "They keep it real."

The audience chuckled.

"So do the bugs flying around."

I smiled.

"Your heart's a really smart thing," Kim began again. "It knows that love is the most important thing in the world.

"Ali and Valerie want to experience the highest level of love. Love with intention, to really put yourself out there and be there for somebody. To really put it on the altar in front of the community. And to have the courage and vulnerability to do it.

"The thing that really impresses me about Ali and Valerie is they make it look simple."

Kim looked at me, and my heart swelled with love. We both smiled through teary eyes.

"We bonded over a strawberry," Kim said to the audience. "That's why I'm up here."

More chuckling.

"They have complex lives. Wrinkles on their brains. Vast pasts. A lot has happened to them before they met each other. They have friends from all around the world. Interests. Responsibilities, obligations, commitments.

"At the end of the day, they know how weird this place is and that you better give people some wiggle room.

"We're messy, complex creatures, and if you don't have an open mind, it can get a bit tricky. But they've made it easy for us. They are understanding, forgiving people, and they have a sense of humor.

"And they've created a fantastic space for us to wiggle. And be ourselves and even celebrate ourselves. And I believe that simplicity is a fantastic foundation for this day and every day for the rest of their lives."

Kim read a passage from a Kahlil Gibran text then.

I dabbed my eyes and hugged Kim.

"I'll now hand it over to one of our dearest friends, local poet, the one and only, beautiful Miss Jenny Root."

Kim stepped aside, and Jenny approached. Josh, Ali's best man, adjusted the mic, and she began.

> *Who would we be if we did not give love a second*
> *chance? Perhaps a third ...*

Jenny paused and looked at me.

> *...or a fourth.*

We laughed. Ali was my fourth husband.

> *but at least as many times as it takes to find*
> *the one we're meant now to dance with, the one*
> *who holds us as a river holds the sun*
> *and lets it shine—*

> *All you have to do is picture these two:*

*The fabulous wild man waving his arms
in ecstatic dance, and she who writes,
whose red hair and bright clothes
prism the spectrum of light*

*the same light as glances off the eagles
choosing their mate for life,
who first test each other with death
plunging together toward earth
in a crazy beautiful spiral dare—*

*Have you seen this?
Two eagles cresting high above the rest,
lock talons and dive,
wheeling over and over
in free fall,
in courtship, in courage,
the speed they inhabit
the surrender they offer
the thrill, the risk, the ride
holding each other
with that talon grip, spinning,
wheeling through cloud and mist
past swifts and starlings
with their fancy loops and twists
their descent a testament,
testimony to the power of trust
of faith in full flower, past branches
of green leaves sparkling with gold
that I-will-hold-you-through-all-of-this dive
that causes other birds to waver
but these two hold*

and as the ground rises to meet them
release, and lift, knowing
they've found the one
to soar with.

AFTER THE CRASH OF CLAPPING SUBSIDED, I HUGGED Jenny through my tears.

"She wrote that particularly for this occasion," Kim said.

Jenny walked back to her chair.

"Now, the most important part. We get to hear Ali and Valerie talk about their love for each other."

Kim stepped back and took the mic out of the stand. I handed my bouquet of yellow flowers to Tamara, my maidly-matron-of-honor, and picked up my notes from the altar. Ali and I stepped in front of the altar. Kim held the mic to my lips.

"Ali, my love. In this love letter to you, I wish to declare my place in this universe, in this forest we're standing in, and in front of all of our friends and family.

"And that place is by your side. Taking road trips together, divvying up the house chores, and taking Sunday naps together." My heart raced and pounded. I swallowed and tried to slow my breathy voice.

"I am yours and you are mine, and together we will house many doggies. We will laugh every day and whisper encouragement to each other on dark nights.

"I love you, Ali Ihsan, because your heart is so big, I fit inside." My voice drifted to a whisper on the last word. I held my breath for a moment, willing myself to not cry.

"I vow," I croaked, "to always, always tell you the truth, in my words and in my deeds."

Ali swayed, like he wanted to take me in his arms.

"I vow to never leave you. To never cheat on you. To grow old with you. I vow to always listen to your fears and to hold you when you are sad." I sniffed and blinked so I could see the page.

"I don't vow to never be irritated with you."

He smiled, and our friends laughed.

"But I do vow to always tell you when that happens so that it doesn't swell into something unmanageable.

"I vow intimacy and public displays of affection, and to share my space and time with you.

"I vow excitement, adventure, wrong turns, winter depression, laughs, tender moments, dancing, sex, dog walks, emotional growth, and all my love every day.

"I vow to be vulnerable with you, to open myself up to you, even if I'm scared, because I trust you. I love you.

"And today, I'm thinking ..." I put down my notes and picked up my cell phone. "... of Jackaroo ..."

Ali raised his eyebrows and nodded his head, hands clasped behind his back.

"... and Jack the Sailor, and of their love. *This couple, they got married, so well they did agree, this couple they got married, so why not you and me.*' And you know I had to bring Jerry into it ..."

I pressed play on a song I'd previously queued up, set to just the right spot. I turned it up full max, and I put my phone up to the microphone.

"Yeah!" someone yelled from the audience.

I smiled at Ali, and we shimmied to the music and kissed in front of the altar.

Josh took the mic.

"Do you have something to say?" he asked Ali.

Ali took the mic and squared his shoulders.

"Valerie, if I could give you the sun, the moon and the stars,

I would. But they are not mine. All I can give you is my love."

I swallowed and held my breath again. I touched my heart and nodded in response.

"Unending love," he said. "And I'm giving it to you." He nodded, eyes bright.

"I love you," he said, and leaned forward to kiss me.

We exchanged rings and held each other's hands, facing each other. Kim came to the mic again.

"This is a Turkish tradition in which two lovers share a sweet."

Ali handed me a caramel, and I took a bite. I fed the other half to him, and we held hands again.

"Now the part we've all been waiting for," Kim said.

Ali and I both frantically chewed faster, and our friends laughed. It was good to laugh and be silly among the tears—even if, especially if, they were tears of joy. But maybe caramel wasn't the right choice.

"We're waiting," Kim said.

"And chewing," Tamara said behind me.

We swallowed our treat and smiled at each other.

"You may now kiss the bride," Kim said.

We kissed, everyone clapped, and I stepped on Ali's toe—another Turkish tradition. Whoever steps on the toe of the other is the one *in charge* of the marriage. (He let me.)

"And now you are husband and wife," Kim said.

Tamara handed me my bouquet, Ali clapped along with everyone else, and then I took his arm.

"The bar is now open. Let the games begin," Kim said.

Much whooping ensued, and our friends threw rose petals at us. At the edge of the meadow, we kissed again, and surreptitiously finished chewing our caramels.

happiness

Happiness is a panting, smiling dog
With a gray muzzle and yellow teeth
Named Casey Jones.

He is traversing the back yard hill
In search of berries.

CHAPTER 101
the best one

I dreamt once that, after a long and loving life together, I woke up just as the sun was rising and Ali was dead beside me. We were in our eighties.

"Oh," I said simply.

I slid over closer to him and laid my head on his shoulder, my arm slung over him—the same way I'd done it thousands of times before. And I wept a goodbye.

His death wasn't tragic. Or accidental.

Just simple and quiet, in his sleep.

In his eighties.

I only hoped this came true because the alternative was horrific and shocking. And I'd already lived through that. But not with him. Not with Ali. And with Ali, it would be worse.

Why?

On the surface, I didn't know, but underneath, it was a silty river water mixture of truths. I was older. I loved him more. I'd only, only, only *ever* been myself with him.

It wasn't just that I could *be myself* with him; I *was* myself with him.

And no one else had seen that. Ever. The closest would be Tamara, but Ali had obviously seen more of me than she had.

If Ali didn't see me, if I didn't see myself through Ali's eyes, could I be real?

Would I revert into my shallow, what-would-the-neighbors-think mask? *Would I start lying again?*

Could I *be* me without Ali?

Or did I come into being when I met him?

No.

No, that would be a pretty lie I'd torture myself with after his death.

I would be Me always.

I was Me before Ali, and that's why our relationship was the Best One. The Only One where I'd been myself from beginning to end—whenever that happened.

There had always been Me in the Us.

Maybe there had only been Us in my other relationships, without the Me. Tamara told me once that I threw myself into love—lost myself—and became whomever I thought my boyfriends wanted. There was no Me in the Us-es.

Ali was the Only One I'd been Me with. That I'd been Real with. And that meant—*could that mean?*—that our relationship was the only Real one I'd ever had.

So, what were the others?

They were real, too, in the way that our relationships happened. They existed. I learned and grew from them. I was even happy in them. But none had been the Best One.

And that's why Ali was the Only One.

He was the Best One.

(*Truth.*)

CHAPTER 102
and then there was me

The great news was I had control over my honesty and the quality of my life. I'd always had that. But now I paid attention to it. I'd learned the same lesson over and over. Honesty was at the core of that.

If I didn't lie to myself (and that meant checking in with journaling and meditation regularly), then I didn't live false lives or live at odds with my Truth.

And therein lay the peace and happiness.

And when I was Real, real stuff happened to me.

Like Real Love.

Like Ali.

But first there was my Truth.

And *then* there was Me.

There always had been.

I just had to stop lying to Her.

author's note

A few years ago, a neighbor of mine said something like, "I try to think about what I want in my life, not necessarily about the money it will take to get it there." The idea being that sometimes, if you are very clear about what you want to manifest, it shows up. Money or not.

So I asked myself that morning all those years ago, "What is it I want in my life?"

And what showed up in my journal that day was .... a personal mission statement.

TOTALLY not what I set out to do, but I was surprised and delighted it showed up.

And on days when I need cheering up, I re-read my mission statement from years ago and realize how perfect-for-me my life really is now (in December 2017 as I write this) (and again in November 2022 as I edit this), and how—pretty much without trying—I live this manifested mission statement every day. Here it is. An affirming mission statement.

It is safe to evolve and I have the emotional courage to do so. I have patience and compassion for myself and others, and I surround myself with people that extend those qualities to me.

I have a strong sense of purpose, fed by my intuition.

I live in a place where I am grounded to the Earth, feel a kinship with the People, and am connected to Source.

I have friends that nurture and support me—some of which I can see socially a couple of times a week. My friends are emotionally courageous people, too, and my relationship with my children includes joy, respect, unconditional love, and nurturing supportive availability.

My life is filled with curiosity, vitality, variety, zest, and writing inspiration. I have financial safety.

I have an artistic and attentive lover and partner that I feel passion and respect and love love love for; and he for me. He evolves and grows with me, alongside me. We challenge and encourage each other.

I have meaningful work that exists in symbiotic support of my life's purpose.

I feed my soul every day.

What's your personal mission statement? Email Valerie@valerieihsan.com and let me know.

author's note 2

What follows is a short piece I wrote originally as a synopsis for the book, before I structured it the way you see today. Then, it became the introduction to the book. And then I was going to chuck it altogether. But something kept me from doing that. Maybe just ego and vanity. Maybe I just wanted you to read it. But it doesn't matter if you do. Because it's really about *you*, the reader. The book is about what you think it is. I wrote the parts that resonate with you just for you. But just in case you want to know, this is what *I* think the book is about:

You Can't Dance a Lie is about a woman (me!) who is afraid of being herself lest she be judged and rejected. So she stays in relationships longer than is good for her—not having the courage to be herself and find love and happiness. *Find* herself, *become* herself more fully in her relationships, rather than slowly morphing into someone she's not to please her man.

She tries mightily to conquer this personal fault that encases her like a shell. She forces her way through, pecking and chipping, shoving first one shoulder through and leaving her husband, then retreating back in the shell in a panic, back into another relationship that doesn't suit her. Doesn't fill her, doesn't bring out the essence of Valerie—perhaps because she never took the time to truly know herself, always living the life she thought others wanted for her, down to the way she cared about things and her opinions on lifestyles and hobbies.

One day she ventured out—and finally, able to push all the way out of the shell, hatched anew into the woman she was at her core. Whole. Alert. Herself. And she left that relationship, too. A haunting one that was mostly fantasy, lived from afar, across the country, and had never fully suited her.

Peeling back the layers, washing off the yolk-sac stickiness, Valerie became Valerie. *Valerian*. The strong one. The valiant.

And because she finally knew herself—when all remnants of shell were gone—she met a man she could truly be herself with. The only man, it turns out, she needed all along. The best man she'd ever been with. Because he was the only man who ever knew her. Truly. Because he was the only man she'd been with after having discovered and befriended herself. Her true self. Her *Truth* self.

dear reader,

Thanks so so much for reading *You Can't Dance a Lie*. I hope you laughed or cried or saw yourself in some of it.

If you enjoyed the book, please do me a HUGE favor and leave a review on your favorite online bookstore's website. It really makes a big difference to see those reviews. It helps others find the book and know it has value, and it helps me to get marketing for the book. Some promotional places won't accept a book on their list if it doesn't have enough reviews.

So, please, if you'd like to help this small business owner (that's me!) and author, please leave a review. Even just a star rating is great.

Blessings,

Valerie Ihsan

free offer

TWO EXCLUSIVE ESSAYS

Oh, the woes of grocery shopping and finding time to write in the summer.

Valerie battles with everyday tasks, like getting her kids to stop with the video-gaming already!, gardening, and making meaning in the mundane. **Download these irreverent, cheeky (and somehow still poignant) essays today.**

acknowledgments

Thanks to my lovely friend, poet **Jenny Root**, for writing such a beautiful homage to my and Ali's love for our wedding ceremony. It still hangs in my office above a silk painting of Krishna and Radha in my Love Corner.

Thanks to **Tamara LeRoy**, my Soul Sister, who tells me like it is and holds me accountable, and who will always love me no matter who or where we are.

Thanks to **Clover Hayes** and **Robert Willman** for teaching me about direct communication, magic, tolerance, patience, and how to rejoice in neuro-divergence. I love you both more than you'll probably ever know. I'm so proud of you. Always and forever. No matter what.

Thanks to my community at TheAuthorLife.com, my editor **Kathrese McKee** at WritingPursuits.com, and for mentors **J. Thorn, Joanna Penn,** and **Rachael Herron**; and local writer friends: **Jo Bartlett, Anthony St. Clair,** and **Erick Mertz**. Thanks for holding me up while I wrote this book.

Thank you to **all my patrons** at Patreon.com/valerieihsan, but especially **Tamara Sue LeRoy, Kimberly George, Sean Sharp,** and **Mary Van Everbroeck.**

And, to My One and Only, **Ali Ihsan Özgenç**. *Seni Seviyorum.* Thank you for loving all of me and inspiring me to be my best self. (*Truth.*)

also by valerie ihsan

Memoir
Smell the Blue Sky: Young, Pregnant, and Widowed

Fiction
The Scent of Apple Tea

Non-Fiction
How to Grieve: Even When You Don't Want To

about the author

Valerie Ihsan is the author of <u>The Scent of Apple Tea</u> and <u>Smell the Blue Sky: Young, pregnant, and widowed</u>, **winner of a B.R.A.G. Medallion for Top Indie-Published Books**. She co-chaired the Eugene Chapter of Willamette Writers for ten years; and podcasts, coaches, and edits for authors. She's served in the United States Army, owns land in Costa Rica, and lives with her husband and three dogs in Springfield, Oregon. She loves chocolate, cheese, and dogs.

Copyright 2022

Library of Congress Control Number: 2022921593

Willow Bench Books

Springfield, Oregon

World of Warcraft ® and Warcraft ® are registered trademarks of Blizzard Entertainment, Inc.

Webkinz ® is a registered trademark of Ganz Midwest-CBK LLC (also known as Ganz).

Wii is a registered trademark of Nintendo of America Inc.

www.ingramcontent.com/pod-product-compliance
Lightning Source LLC
Chambersburg PA
CBHW030430010526
44118CB00011B/576